THE NEW TRADITIONAL

Copyright © 2008 by Darryl Carter Media Group, LLC

All rights reserved.
Published in the United States by Clarkson Potter/Publishers, an imprint of
the Crown Publishing Group, a division of Random House, Inc., New York.
www.crownpublishing.com
www.clarksonpotter.com

Clarkson N. Potter is a trademark and Potter and colophon are registered
trademarks of Random House, Inc.

Library of Congress Cataloging-in-Publication Data
Carter, Darryl, 1961–
    The new traditional : reinvent-balance-define your home / Darryl Carter.
    — 1st ed.
    1. Interior decoration—Psychological aspects.   I. Title.
NK2113.C37   2008
747.01'9—dc22   2007045663

ISBN 978-0-307-40865-5

Printed in Singapore

Photographs by Gordon Beall

10   9   8   7   6   5   4   3   2   1

First Edition

acknowledgments

Thanks many times over to:

Otis, my sage and now gray hound who has somehow had his picture taken more than I have. My parents, God bless them, for their unwavering support. Mary Haft, my friend, neighbor, and confidant. All of my design studio staff (huge God bless, I'm so sorry), who will hopefully survive this publication. A whole bunch of reasonable and loyal clients; a whole bunch of magazine, newspaper, and television folks; and a whole bunch of lawyers, banks, and accountants. The now very famous Ken Downing for his early belief and support. Maura McEvoy for taking the picture of me that everyone is now tired of seeing. With obvious and special thanks to Gordon Beall, Amanda Correa, Trish Donnally, Gordon Elliot, Aliza Fogelson, Charles Grazioli, Dana Hughens, Sibylle Kazeroid, Christine Mortimer-Biddle, Marysarah Quinn, Roberto Sablayrolles, Mark Smiley, Edward Teplitz, Kim Tyner, Sydney Webber, and Nancy Webster.

And finally, thanks to my near and dear professionally and personally. You know who you are and I was told to limit this to one page, so here's your fifteen minutes: BA, JA, AB, BB, DB, AC, BC, JC, KC, QC, RC, JD, BE, AF, PF, TF, CG, DG, GG, LG, DH, JH, PH, DK, JK, DL, ML, RTL, DM, MM, SM, SM, LO, KP, MP, SP, JR, LR, MR, PR, RR, AS, AS, CS, DS, NS, RS, SS, TS, WS, SU, PV, DW, GW, LW, TW, SY, and IZ.

contents

introduction
follow my example, follow your passion

My design has been characterized as the New Traditional for its unusual pairing of the modern with the antique. Over the years, I have developed a method for choosing and placing objects as I execute a room. Through trial and error my affinity has clearly emerged for classic forms, whether modern or antique. This has been further refined by a specific color palette, along with wood patina, timeworn texture, and a particular appreciation for the importance of uniform scale. Upon reflecting on these elements, I have discovered that an abiding logic distinguishes thoughtful design. Understanding and adhering to this logic invariably results in beautiful, approachable, lasting environments. These environments become even more exceptional when they express individual tastes, outside of, if not in spite of, trend or studied regiment. In order to achieve these remarkable spaces, confidence is critical. In this book I share my design philosophy so that you can make use of it as you set about confidently designing your own home in your own style.

I made a belated career change from law to design. This was prompted by a series of unlikely events that thankfully forced me down an indelible path toward my true passion. Though it was clear early on where my interests would guide me, getting there and finding a sense of comfort was a journey. I grew up being groomed to assume the leadership of my family's business. However, I wanted to do something creative. This was a far-fetched notion among my peers, all of whom were gearing up for future careers in medicine, law, or politics. Frantically preparing to produce Ivy-worthy SAT scores, I was covertly sketching a portfolio for submission to the top design schools in the country. When I received early acceptance into the Rhode Island School of Design, my father grudgingly toured the school while remaining steadfast to his master plan for me. During the tour we walked into a figurative art class—the subject, a nude student at the room's center. Needless to say, my father did not see the point. A liberal arts education would follow. Years later, as preordained, I earned my Juris Doctor and obediently pursued my expected course working for the family business.

I moved into a co-op in a historic landmark building in Washington, D.C., in 1991. This space spoke to me beyond any of its obvious imperfections. Extraordinary architecture was preserved beneath too many layers of paint. Arched casement windows, picture molding, a circular entry foyer, two wood-burning fireplaces, 10-foot ceilings, and an unobstructed cityscape were among the intrigues of the space that would become my laboratory. I was immediately engaged by its potential and set about reinventing it.

In 1997, the apartment was photographed for the coffee-table book *Private Washington*. Later it would appear on the cover of *Metropolitan Home*.

The continued interest these publications garnered was varied and unexpected. In what seemed an instant, I had changed careers. I established my firm, the foundation of which rested upon the support of my parents and some very loyal, if not daring, first clients. Shortly thereafter I began to receive retail inquiries. In 2001, I launched my first furniture collection, for Neiman Marcus Home. The positive reaction to this collection would begin my path into furniture design. In looking back, I can see that this venture grew organically out of my interior decorating commissions. I have been routinely challenged to find and pair contemporary furniture pieces with antiques. Often contemporary furniture is difficult to place due to its scale or inauthentic patina. Antiques conversely present their own challenges. The particular piece that you may need to complete a space may be difficult, if not seemingly impossible, to find: sets of dining chairs may have been separated over the years; scale may be too diminutive for comfort. Reconciling these challenges and accomplishing a thoughtful, livable mix is the object of my design.

If you follow the guidelines offered in this book, you should find yourself confidently creating environments that reflect your individual taste. You will discover that you have produced not only a comfortable refuge but also a lasting, beautiful living environment.

A LIVING SPACE
SERVES AS BOTH
DINING ROOM
AND LIBRARY.

1 adapt
make your home work for you

Your home should be reflective of your personal style. I've found that my most successful collaborations occur with clients who have a strong sense of themselves and their lifestyles. In creating a home, the objective should be to make comfortable environments that uniquely suit you.

Everything we do, even the professions we select, is guided by the affirmation we seek from others. We all have aspirations; this is a by-product of the culture we live in. That said, there are ways to create an inviting environment without compromising yourself for the occasional visitor. For instance, when I talk to a client about the proverbial "dinner party" as I try to gauge his or her entertaining style, I ask, "How often are you really going to have a sit-down dinner for

twenty?" While the dining room is sometimes the best space in the house, it's often the least utilized and may even take on the feel of an empty boardroom. If you rarely host a seated dinner, why not rethink the use of that space?

I helped one client reenvision a large but seldom-used dining room, encouraging her to turn it into a reception parlor or a second living room. I suggested that she might prefer to have an intimate candlelit dinner and a great bottle of wine in a relaxed salon setting lined with bookshelves, as this seemed far more consistent with her thoughtful, engaging, and humorous nature than presiding over a dinner from the head of a 20-foot table. A stilted environment makes everyone self-conscious of his or her every movement and can inhibit comfortable and gracious entertaining. In this case, a small ante-room worked well as a dining room, freeing the original larger space for the client's family's more frequent use as a reading room.

Rather than furnishing your home to respect the expectations of others, identify what works best for your lifestyle.

creating convertible spaces

Where is it written that a particular room in your house has to be used for a singular purpose? I don't have any chairs around my dining room table. The room is far better suited for formal receptions. I'm never going to eat there. When I have friends for dinner, we eat in a solarium adjacent to the kitchen. I always prefer kitchens to formal dining spaces for congregating.

I suggest designing rooms for maximum use. For example, I converted a remote room on the top floor of my Washington, D.C., residence into a welcoming guest room/library. I don't have guests often enough to justify dedicating the room exclusively to visitors, particularly given its captivating views. This room is crisp with the contrast of white walls, white-stained floors, and a variety of dark wood furniture. A balanced mix of favorite collectibles, many of which are flea-market finds, is in good company with rarefied antiques. Opposing period English daybeds, walls of bookcases, and intriguing park views inspire me.

Dark wood floors were appropriate to the formal architecture throughout, but for this space I wanted an ethereal departure from the rest of the house. The room, given its light and views, is truly reminiscent of a tree house, as intended. As for floor finish, I generally tend toward the extremes: espresso or winter white. Dark floors show scratches, and light floors reveal dust. I remember the sinking feeling the first time my dogs, Otis and Lucy, scratched the floors. It's like that first ding on a new car. You get over it. I'd rather have the invaluable companionship of my dogs than perfect floors.

In my country house, all the floors were painted with white porch paint. I purposely designed my kitchen there to feel distinctly different from my kitchen in the city, integrating open rustic shelving of reclaimed barn wood. A diminutive door in its original weathered white paint, reclaimed from a historic farmhouse, conceals the pantry.

A LIBRARY WITH A PAIR OF DAYBEDS MAKES AN ATTRACTIVE REFUGE THAT WELCOMES THE OCCASIONAL GUEST.

I WHITEWASHED THE
FLOORS IN MY GUEST
ROOM/LIBRARY TO
CONTRAST
WITH THE DARK
FURNITURE AND
UNDERSCORE THE
SENSE OF SPACE.
THE WING CHAIR OF
MY DESIGN IS
COVERED IN
DURABLE FAUX
LEATHER.

A MARBLE-TOPPED
ITALIAN LIBRARY TABLE
WITH HIDDEN DRAWERS
IS A FUNCTIONAL
WORK SPACE WITH
STORAGE FOR CUTLERY.
LIKEWISE, IT SERVES
AS A CANOPY FOR
FEATHER DOG BEDS.

finding perfection in imperfection

We are too preoccupied with perfection. Sometimes imperfection is a relief, inviting use and adding character to a space. It sets a posture of ease, while a pristine room signals caution. What I'm suggesting is that you live in your space. Signs of life are good design elements. Rugs that have worn from traffic, scratches on floors, and nicks on baseboards are all forgivable, if not welcome. This sensibility holds true with antiques as well. I rarely have antiques restored, because I prefer the patina that comes with life. The wear on a piece of furniture invites its continued use. The timeworn farm table in my kitchen illustrates this. Because the table has survived more than a century of discernible wear, a guest does not need to be nervous about setting a glass on it for fear of leaving a water ring. Don't buy anything so precious that you're afraid people will break, stain, scratch, or sit on it.

A WEATHERED
FARMHOUSE DOOR
ADDS AUTHENTICITY
TO THE PANTRY.
THE NEW CEMENT
FIREPLACE SURROUND
IS EXECUTED IN A
PERIOD FINISH.

IN ITS UPRIGHT
POSITION, THIS FARM
TABLE WOULD SERVE AS
AN IDEAL BENCH FOR
BOOT REMOVAL IN A
MUD ENTRY.

THE LINEAR
GEOMETRY OF THE FLOOR
INTEGRATES WITH THE
SPHERICAL CEMENT
ARCHITECTURAL FINIALS.

personalizing your home

Another key element to creating a comfortable home is to incorporate elements that reflect your interests. I'm fascinated with geometry, so it is often integrated into my design. In my city home, the entry foyer stair is a remarkably graceful series of planes that guides one through the entire house. The picture molding beneath the stair was simplified, clearly delineating a triangle. A linear bronze pedestal I commissioned, topped with three spherical architectural finials, accents the stairwell. The doorway for the black milled door beneath the stairs was heightened to be consistent with the original door openings elsewhere in the foyer. While the original mahogany handrail remains, I replaced the visually cumbersome Georgian wood pickets, which were three per stair, with narrower forged metal pickets, now two per stair. The foyer floor previously consisted of intricate, 1 by 6-inch wood strips, laid individually by hand in a basket-weave pattern. To honor the tradition of the house while modernizing it, the floor was replaced with 24 by 24-inch tiles of honed limestone, which were scored to suggest four narrow, single tiles that had been laid in a basket-weave pattern. The wood baseboards were replaced with limestone block. In addition to reflecting my penchant for geometry, the overall effect creates a sense of calm and order.

Decorating should be an inspiring, creative process. Don't let an overwhelming monotony or lack of self-expression overtake your home as it does in so many interiors. There is no reason for this to happen. Every city has a wealth of resources for home furnishings, from the independent art dealer representing emerging art to inner-city thrift stores to the rarefied antiques dealer. No one should settle for an uninteresting environment. Much of the static that emerges in so many houses stems from a lack of invention and a lack of confidence to mix different objects, styles, finishes, and types of wood. People don't take chances.

A FORMER POOL AREA, REDEFINED AS AN OUTDOOR LIVING ROOM, SEASONALLY ACCOMMODATES INTIMATE GATHERINGS AROUND THE FIRE.

An overwhelming universal I encounter when I first arrive at a client's home is "sameness." Some years ago as I glanced out of my window into an adjacent apartment building, a poignant graphic was etched into my memory. I was struck by the placement of furnishings, albeit different objects of the same sort, in all the same locations on all the west-facing floors from one to sixteen. It was as though each apartment was subject to a prescribed furniture layout plan.

Lifestyle should be contemplated well before the acquisition of furniture pieces. This may require innovation in terms of how you use the spaces in your home, including those on the exterior. Many of my clients have labored over a decision about whether to move or perhaps redefine their existing living spaces. A move is, without fail, an unpleasant proposition, if only for the logistics; so it's encouraging to think that the home you live in can be remodeled to suit your needs. One memorable project involved clients who had a lovely home that became increasingly challenging as the family grew. Their inner-city town house, which was landlocked, could not be expanded; but they had a veritable oasis in the form of a rear garden, which had not been exploited to its full capacity. Their true need was not for day-to-day living space, but rather for a commodious environment for their large-scale entertaining. The garden was lovely, but the existing lap pool presented a hazard for the children and occupied a great deal of potentially usable entertaining space. I had the pool removed, and the evolution of the space from a garden to an outdoor living, dining, and entertaining space was exciting to bring to reality. I commissioned a casual stone-block terrace centered around a magnificent outdoor fireplace that would accommodate a viable outdoor living and dining area and serve seasonally for a variety of entertaining needs. The pool was filled in, the retaining walls were skimmed with stucco, and an architectural pergola and overscaled planters for future vining were added. Mature boxwoods completed the space.

Along with the need for an entertaining venue, clients increasingly request a fully functioning office in the home. Ideally this is a dual-purpose space that remains consistent with the design sense of the rest of the home. The obvious antidote here is to use beautiful, traditional furniture pieces adaptively, so they can accommodate work functions. A drop-leaf table with both leaves up, flanked by two armchairs, can make a great desk. An antique armoire can be retrofitted as a desk with the addition of pocket doors and a pull-out tray for a computer keyboard. A file cabinet can be sequestered behind a decorative screen, which will not preclude its accessibility. Serving a

THE NINETEENTH-CENTURY
GATELEG TABLE MAKES
AN ATTRACTIVE WORK
SURFACE IN LIEU OF A
TRADITIONAL DESK.

utilitarian function, home work spaces often have untapped potential as convertible entertaining spaces. In one case, I designed an old-world library replete with custom millwork and bookcases. I ornamented the ceiling with heavy coffers and designed an imposing cast-concrete mantel for the fireplace. At the room's center, I placed a nineteenth-century gateleg table topped with an antique globe and flanked by two vintage Chesterfield sofas. I added an antique armoire, two large paneled screens, and a bench. For entertaining, the client simply removes the rolling office chair, closes the armoire, drops the sides of the gateleg table, and slides the screens back into place.

Another option is to employ a seldom-used guest room to support the home office or library, which works if thoughtfully executed. A client wanted to plan for the occasional overnight guest. Space was at a premium, however, so a dedicated guest room was impractical. Sometimes a solution may be so obvious that we fail to consider it or perhaps we stigmatize a would-be solution with a predisposition or a finite visual image. Consider old methods with new execution. For some reason the Murphy bed immediately conjures images of a mildewed, roadside motel on the way to a not-so-fancy beach. I can be this specific because this was my preconceived idea until I needed a small-space solution that could be achieved only by the addition of a Murphy bed.

A FORMER WORKTABLE SERVES AS A DECORATIVE SIDEBOARD IN A GUEST BEDROOM.

The style was midcentury modern in a prewar co-op. The Beaux Arts vocabulary of the building had been maintained in the apartment and could not be compromised. The would-be guest room had one of the best views in the apartment, so it did not take much to convince the owner to locate the home office in this space. But where would a visitor stay? Only one interior wall would accommodate a bed, and only if the cavity for the bed claimed some of the interior of an adjacent closet. A regular bed or a sleep sofa would not fit in the space. A Murphy bed was constructed that when retracted was indiscernible from the existing mill pattern of the walls. A primitive textile mounted under thin Plexiglas was permanently mounted on the wall of the Murphy bed's milled underside.

the last word

Making your home work for you is an evolutionary process, as your needs may change over time. Explore ways to maximize the potential of different rooms. Tailor your home to suit your lifestyle.

A SHALLOW NINETEENTH-
CENTURY APOTHECARY
CHEST PROVIDES
CONVENIENT
STORAGE.

A RECLAIMED
BARN DOOR
CONCEALS A
TELEVISION. THE
RUSH SEAT OF A
REFINED CHAIR
COMPLEMENTS
THIS SETTING.

2 define

identify your style, then forget the rules

Good interior design is subjective. The most important criterion for successful design is that it provide comfort. If you adopt this criterion, you will overcome two of the most recurrent impediments to honest design: fear of making a wrong decision and preoccupation with the approval of others. Whether you are designing your home yourself or working with a professional, considering comfort is essential to creating a home that is true to your real needs.

A design professional will not be able to successfully create a pleasing environment for a client without a full understanding of the client's lifestyle needs. Communicating these may be more difficult than it sounds. In my experience, this process is much like the dance enacted in any other intimate relationship, through which familiarity and dialogue grow deeper over time. Once you have established your parameters, leave the design to the professional. Most important, do not enlist third-party opinions. That will only add confusion and stifle the process. Keep this in mind as you discuss your home with your designer. If you are working without a designer, this book will strengthen your confidence as you decorate your home and develop your own sense of style.

I always know when my clients and I have reached the defining point in our relationship. As in any relationship, you have to feel out your partner. Most often this translates into developing a heightened sensitivity about what offends, and tiptoeing around that subject. What a relief it is when everyone finally gets comfortable. Nothing is more liberating than truthful, fluid dialogue. The first time a client says "I hate it," I know there is trust. Nothing is more counterproductive in this process than gratuitous deference. If the client actually does hate something, the challenge is to thoughtfully accommodate his or her feedback while retaining the design's intent. Good design begins by quelling predisposition. I am thankful for such a varied client portfolio. The diversity of taste has been indispensable in broadening my vocabulary and increasing my appreciation for options I had originally overlooked.

In working with interiors ranging from Indo-Chinese to Tudor, I've encountered almost *every* style. I learned early on that it was foolhardy to try to impose my tastes on my clients. The art is to discern, through careful listening, the repetitive common denominators and aesthetic preferences expressed by the client and refine them into a design. In other words, my task is to distinguish what clients really want from what they may think they want at the inception, and then to translate their desires into a stylish, functional environment.

While there are no rules of taste, there is a logic that helps create a comfortable, cohesive environment. This entails a disciplined thought process, which is the essence of this book. I believe my fluid design philosophy was born of the early need in my career to respond to a variety of client tastes. This was the logical aftermath of much of my experimenting with different styles in my own

MODERN RESIDES
WITH ANTIQUE.

living spaces. As I mentioned, a former apartment that served as a design laboratory was featured in my first published work. Upon reflection, I am not certain I would decorate it now as I did then. I find myself critical of some of its design elements. I never dislike what I have done before, but as my vocabulary and vision expand, I see how things could be improved. I say this to reassure anyone who has ever doubted him- or herself when it comes to a design decision. The appreciation of design is an ever-evolving process: The more exposure you have, the more you seek, and the more you broaden and refine your tastes. That is how it should be approached. As with any educational process, there are no bad ideas or foolish questions.

Experiment; you may discover unexpected rewards. For instance, I intuitively place modern furniture with antiques. I find an eclectic mix of objects more faithful to individual tastes. Rooms of this sort take on far greater character than rooms filled with formulaic suites of matching furniture. While mixing different styles and periods of furniture can be daunting, logic will see you through. I first suggest approaching the space through a lens of geometry. Regard the furniture pieces as shapes and sizes that make sense together. All furniture is derivative; the modern is inspired by the antique, so it is logical that they should reside in harmony. For instance, Early American furniture, graceful in line and free of superfluous ornamentation, is quite modern relative to some of its more highly carved European contemporaries.

your design vocabulary

Once you've studied your environment and limited your design universe to elements that are visually inspiring, this language will become the vocabulary of your home. Is it natural and rustic? Slick and modern? The answers to these questions are the substance of your design vocabulary. To begin defining your style, study interior design books and shelter magazines, earmarking pages that appeal to you. I encourage all my clients to do this. Magazine clippings present a veritable Rorschach test. I've found that what appears to be an unrelated collection of clippings presents a cohesive mosaic of taste when carefully examined. If your spouse or partner is involved in the decision-making process, both of you should maintain separate files of clippings and subcategorize them from broad to specific. Make files for individual rooms; for interior and exterior architecture; for landscaping, pools, and gardens.

Study the elements within the pictures. You'll find that there are common denominators among them. You may discover that the furnishings are not consistent from one clipping to the next but that all the rooms you gravitate toward have a wash of certain colors. This is your preferred color palette. Or there may be a type of furniture you're attracted to in pictures of rooms that are otherwise disparate. Try to determine what factors attract you. Do you respond consistently to more elaborate interiors or to clean-lined ones? Are you drawn to silk and satin window treatments or to less structured linens? Do you prefer matte to shiny, wood to metal, traditional to contemporary, or "masculine" to "feminine"? Are you responding to the warmth in a room, the composition, or the texture of rough-hewn surfaces? Is it the patina and character of an old farm table that appeals to you? Or is it the gravity of the table's size as an anchor in the room? Are you fond of more intimate spaces with furnishings that are more diminutive and delicate in scale?

CONTRASTS ADD DIMENSION AND FLOW BETWEEN MEDIA AND LIVING SPACES.

DURABLE
MATERIALS WERE
ORGANIC TO THIS
SUMMER STUDIO,
WHICH INCLUDES
AN ALLOY TABLE.

40

Once you have identified these common threads, you are well on your way to establishing your design preferences. This process will continually be refined from the broad to the specific. Whether you prefer rustic or modern style will dictate which finishes and textiles, window treatments, and furnishings will work best. Chrome, for instance, is an example of a slick finish that would be more commonly used in a modern setting. Woven tapestry textiles would perhaps relate more to the rustic. In general, your vocabulary will consist of the words and phrases you use to describe the collection of colors, fabrics, textures, shapes, compositions, and finishes that satisfy your taste and stand the test of time. This is by no means intended to suggest that environments be overstudied. The appropriate mixture of styles is what makes an environment outstanding; but there should also be continuity.

Clarify your likes so you can articulate them. Call the owners of the house you've always admired and ask them the name of the exterior paint color. I remember spending weeks tracking down a rector in a remote town where I had driven past a quaint church that was painted in the most unusual shade of Pommery mustard yellow. Doing so was still probably more efficient than putting twenty different paint strikes up on the exterior of my clients' home to try to show them the shade I had in mind. Establishing a color vocabulary is particularly difficult given the number of options. It's important to be able to say "green" to your spouse, a general contractor, and a designer and have each of them understand what "green" is to you.

A MODERN
INTERPRETATION
OF A PRIMITIVE
RAG RUG IS
BALANCED BY THE
ENGLISH REGENCY
GIRANDOLE
MIRROR CIRCA
1810.

collaboration and compromise

If there's a partnership in your home, approach this exercise of clipping tear sheets, studying them, and developing your own personal design wish list as recreation rather than as a game to be won. Where you were once at odds, you may discover common likes. This process will help facilitate an understanding of your partner's taste as well as your own. A dialogue about why you like certain things will result in a more harmonious outcome than a demand would. When two or more people are involved in the decorating process, establish order among the decision makers. There needs to be some sort of parity and there needs to be some organization. Decide who has better spatial sense. One may have a better sense of architecture. One may have a better sense of style. Likewise, one may have a better sense of color or scale. Agree on where the talent lies and hand over control. Then all egos are assuaged and productive boundaries have been established.

Be realistic when working with others. Agree from the start that, at times, you'll disagree. In other words, be prepared to compromise. Processing information and translating it into a singular or shared vocabulary will take some ingenuity, but the outcome is often brilliant design innovation. This is the type of interplay I use to collaborate with my clients.

When living in a space over a long period of time, you may develop a regimen of how you exist in that space, and it is very possible that a redefinition will serve all the same needs a move would address. You may be surprised to find that solutions are often obvious. You may in fact find that you don't need more space, but rather a greater sense of space.

An interior room may feel oppressive due to an absence of natural light, when just outside that room may be a lovely garden view with a southern exposure that could lend light and charm to the space. Even an existing window may present an opportunity to add more light: The enlarging of a window opening by a few feet often brings an appreciable increase of light into a space. A double-hung window might be replaced with a full-height casement window or French doors. Access to an exterior view, immediate or distant, may also greatly enhance the sense of space within an interior room. Even if the exterior view is not the most interesting, it can often be improved through landscaping or plantings. Existing doors may be expanded with side lights or transoms. Upper-floor rooms may benefit from the addition of decorative wrought-iron balconies.

The uppermost floor of a home with low or pitched ceilings might be ripe for redefinition. Instead of being relegated as storage space, it can serve as a home office, guest room, or play area with the addition of dormers, which may also enhance the exterior appeal of the home if appropriately executed. Even in smaller areas such as upper-floor bathrooms, you could add a pinwheel oculus for more light if the exterior architecture allows it. In a bath or powder room, these are typically placed higher than a standard window to help preserve privacy.

Interior ceiling heights may be optically adjusted through a number of ceiling treatments that suggest greater height but do not in fact require raising an existing ceiling. The general goal of any of these executions is to accentuate the ceiling discreetly, but enough that you become more conscious of its integration into the entire architectural envelope. The addition of coffers or an attractive ceiling detail may serve this end. A tin ceiling in a kitchen can be painted in the wall color for an interesting architectural blending effect that fits the style of the home. These options may be preferable when there are existing structural or utility prohibitions that preclude raising the ceiling.

My design penchant is as much for the modern as for the antique, so a number of my commissions involve couples who have significantly different tastes. The solution may boil down to creating a modern envelope to satisfy one partner's needs for sparingly furnished spaces and the other's desire for antique-filled rooms. Conversely, a period architectural

DELICATE LINES
REFINE THIS
COTTAGE
BEDROOM.

THE CURVE OF A
WING CHAIR
LENDS GRACE IN
THIS LINEAR
SPACE.

vocabulary, for example, could be balanced by a large, modern art canvas. Include small gestures of a similar juxtaposition progressively throughout the design process, and you'll realize with relief that these presumably contrary aesthetics can live together quite harmoniously.

Differences in taste may arise in more than just furniture styles. Partners' color preferences often differ, too. Once again, the obvious solution may not be so obvious. I have encountered this situation so many times that I have a ready solution, a literal compromise: Choose a universe of colors that make sense together, and water them down so that they merely suggest their vibrant counterparts. Agree on which of these colors can be used to punctuate the environment and use the more outstanding incarnation as a leading edge on a drape, the faint element of pattern in a rug, a subtle detail on a pillow, or a hint of velvet on a small piece of occasional furniture such as a footstool. Use paint to modernize a space. A room filled with antiques that is wallpapered may produce a staid sensibility, while those same furnishings set against a monochrome paint palette may appear more modern as the architecture of the furniture becomes more pronounced as sculpture. Or use paint to neutralize architectural embellishments. Dark, heavy, oppressive woods may be uplifted when painted a light color.

Consider alternatives to the obvious solutions when problem solving in your home. In my farmhouse I was steadfast in my desire to create an environment that would accommodate muddy boots as well as muddy dogs. I frankly struggled over this, because my true penchant is for very clean design. Perhaps because there was no client to impose practical parameters, despite all my efforts to use forgiving barnyard plaid and noncommittal driftwood flooring, the space was destined to end up being entirely white, as it did. Once I finally accepted this reality, the challenge was to execute this aesthetic in a user-friendly fashion. I used a quick fix: durable finishes that happened to be white. In effect, I whitewashed the entire interior structure. The original structure of the house was preserved and the character maintained, through the use of common color, which unified the antique structure with the contemporary. This created a very open and serene sense—wholly consistent with the way I wanted to feel while in the house.

My approach to this property was unorthodox, and I have to say I was apprehensive about painting over some of the existing beautifully patinated finishes, but maintaining them would have defeated the visual serenity of a weekend getaway. I also think the house spoke to me in such a way that this was the appropriate treatment. The irony here? The period farmhouses I had so romanticized in theory were, in fact, generally light-deprived given their low ceilings, small rooms, and deep windowsills, all features typical of primitive farmhouse architecture. The truth is they all felt like a rainy day. The house that I finally bought, though built in the mid–nineteenth century, had a light-filled contemporary addition. As it turned out, the light was very important to me as I contemplated actually living in the space. The discrepancy between historical examples and my farmhouse presented the best of all worlds. It was easier for me to rationalize making the contemporary addition look and feel old. Though I probably could not articulate this at the time, that is why I place such emphasis on being true to your tastes and lifestyle. How you feel in a house is the most critical consideration.

the last word

Observe the elements of your home that speak to you and find a way to bring them forth. Use your newfound vocabulary to express precisely what you're thinking.

MOLDING WAS
USED TO CREATE
AN OVERDOOR TO
MATCH THE
HIGHER EXISTING
DOOR OPPOSITE
THE PUBLIC
HALLWAY.

3 envelop

build the envelope by adding architectural details

Carefully examining a space before furnishing it is critical. Creating a proper envelope requires as much care as does the decorating. It is essential to address ceilings, floors, walls, windows, and doors at the outset. In fact, if you treat these elements thoughtfully to begin with, you may save time, trouble, and resources in the long run. Fewer furniture pieces are necessary in an environment that has been sensitively enhanced through the addition of appropriate architectural elements. Sometimes what seems like an inconsequential detail changes the entire look of a room. Adding texture to floors, coffering ceilings, painting walls with a hint of color, enhancing windows architecturally by adding simple wood embellishments, cosmetically raising headers on doors, and building bookcases are among the ways to improve the envelope of a room.

Whether you're considering new construction or a renovation, think about the potential of a room and analyze exactly how you intend to use that room daily. This will facilitate detailed advance planning, which will in turn save time and money and obviate the need for future changes. Changing the floor stain after the fact, for instance, is a labor-intensive and dusty proposition.

treating floors

Consider floor stain much as you do wall color, but if you're looking at a home in its entirety, floors are perhaps more important than walls as they unify the space. Lighten floors to make a space feel more open. Darken them to make a space feel more intimate. This decision may be driven simply by the amount of light in a room. A first step in establishing the vocabulary of your home is deciding whether to whitewash or darken floors. Medium and pattern may also add dimension to flooring. Though often used in bathrooms, stone can make a space very sterile, absent an innovative execution. Consider adding texture through the use of pattern. Laying stone in a herringbone pattern, for instance, may lend old-world charm. I did this in my own bath as it was consistent with the two side-by-side, freestanding vintage tubs; the farm-table vanity; and government-issue barrister cabinets that serve as towel storage. A garden-variety marble floor laid in a typical fashion would have been static in this setting.

Baseboard treatment can also make an appreciable difference. Use a 6- to 8-inch stone base mold; this adds great architectural presence, whenever you are placing like stone flooring. If you have high ceilings, this is a very subtle but significant enhancement to a room.

enhancing ceilings

Occasionally, replacing less-than-ideal elements may not be possible. I was once challenged by a pink terra-cotta floor in a sunroom and adjoining kitchen that the clients were not willing to replace given the required demolition. In this instance, architectural embellishments were thoughtfully used to distract. Bookshelves were installed at the perimeter of the sunroom. The heavy crown molding at the tops of these bookshelves supported beams suspended above windows that together created the sense of the spine of an attic.It was as though there was a pergola at the room's center. Ceilings are a major intrigue for me. It's inexpensive to add a few beams or bead board to a ceiling. In this instance, directing attention away from the terra-cotta floor by improving the ceiling was a great foil.

Architecturally, I prefer to dispense with superfluous bells and whistles. I have removed contractor-grade egg-and-dart molding on more than one occasion. Strive for authenticity, not grandeur. Remove elaborate crown molding and replace it with simple, rounded cove molding. This will subtly enhance ceiling heights without overwhelming a room.

Architectural detail that you add or subtract should appropriately enhance the setting. Rather than a heavily embellished rosette above a chandelier, a simple one in a traditional room reads as a thoughtful though innocuous detail. Rosettes are available in plaster or a variety of lightweight synthetics. Once painted, they can be easily mounted on the ceiling.

rethinking walls

Be true to the architectural style of the space and create a harmonious envelope. I tend to prefer simple paint to other wall treatments. In some cases, wallpaper is the appropriate choice. When a setting calls for wall embellishment beyond paint, consider adding picture molding to walls. Wallpaper works well in smaller spaces, such as hallways, powder rooms, formal coat closets, bays, and alcoves. It can add an element of surprise to an otherwise neutral environment. Think of the silk lining in a bespoke suit; it is personal and indulgent at once. I suggest using timeless wallpapers such as painted grass cloths, Egyptian linens, matte crackle, or tea-stained toiles.

Depending on the project setting, I may have a doorway heightened to enhance the sense of space, or moved to accommodate large art canvases. Occasionally it is wise to remove a wall altogether to create larger rooms. Conversely, if a room feels uncomfortably large, add walls to create more intimate areas within the space. Consider adding a wall of French doors to bisect a space that feels too big. I did this in my kitchen and accomplished two goals: I reduced the size of the kitchen to a more livable scale while creating an adjacent breakfast area that has the sense of a conservatory. The wall with three sets of interior French doors mirrors an opposing wall of doors that leads to a terrace. Coffered ceilings were also added. Architectural balance, for my purposes, is achieved when each wall in a room has a similar noncompeting visual interest. Once this is attained, only simple gestures are required in the way of furnishings. An antique baker's rack, a weathered farm table, and a functional apothecary cabinet serve this space perfectly.

lengthening windows

If your windows aren't full height or if you have odd-size windows next to each other or windows that don't provide much of a view, shutters can camouflage unappealing architecture, diffuse light, and create symmetry.

In my bath, for instance, I had low, unattractive windows that overlooked a light well between my home and the neighboring town house. I added full-height shutters that start at the inset at the top of the windows and extend to the floor, and framed them with molding. The louvered part of the shuttered doors extends to the base of the windows so that light is diffused naturally, while the bottom third of the doors, which are concealing the wall, are solid recessed panels. The shutters create the illusion of full-height doors that lead to a balcony.

Another way to improve a window with nominal cost is to add decorative molding. If the window is high, add decorative molding directly below it. If the window is low, add decorative molding directly above it. This will visually lengthen the window. Paint the window molding the same color as other door surrounds in the room. The once-awkward window will then be consistent with the rest of the openings.

statement doors

Changing a door height and the door itself can make a dramatic difference. With adjustments, odd door heights can be reconciled. If a door leading into a dining room is higher than the kitchen door opposite, adding milled overdoors or glass transoms to the shorter door will make it read the same height as the taller one. Follow the same principle when you want to visually lengthen a window. Use decorative molding to build a panel above the door, then frame it with molding to match the existing door casing. In a more modern setting, simply use drywall or plaster and add a clean-lined panel above the door. This will create the illusion of height. This technique is particularly effective where there are lower ceilings. Choose doors that are appropriate to the architecture. Nothing appeals more than sliding planes of glass in the proper modern context. But in a more traditional home, they don't make sense. Mullioned French doors are more appropriate, especially where existing windows are of the same character.

Just as door treatment can improve the overall sense of a room, unobtrusive hardware also lends longevity. Consider using levers instead of knobs. They can be more graceful in appearance. When it comes to hardware, I generally stick with the classics. Don't choose things that are too of the moment. When you make a decision, even one as seemingly simple as door hardware, be sure that you will be able to live with it for several years. Bronze, nickel, chrome, and porcelain are classic finishes that will stand up to the test of time.

bookshelves: the most intimate architectural detail

There may be no more intimate architectural detail than the bookshelf. Books add vital character to a room. They unabashedly reveal the home owner's interests. The challenge in a space filled with bookcases is to avoid clutter. Rather than completely lining bookshelves with books, use some shelves to display art, including sculpture, antiques, vintage maps, primitive pieces like masks or pre-Columbian artifacts, and other collectibles.

BOOKSHELVES LEND INTIMACY TO THIS QUAINT GUEST ROOM.

A MODERN
CREMONE BOLT
ENHANCES THE
CHARACTER OF A
GLASS LIBRARY-
CABINET DOOR.

unexpected benefits

Sometimes changing one element of the envelope can have multiple benefits. While renovating a client's home, for example, I wanted to coffer the living room ceiling to add architectural interest and increase the ceiling height. But the existing ductwork was running on the diagonal across the room. Although the client didn't want to replace the existing ductwork, due to the inconvenience and expense, rerouting the ducts to the perimeter of the room—without having to replace the existing heating and air-conditioning system—solved the problem. The benefit to adding a coffered ceiling was increased ceiling height at the room's center and access to adjacent ceiling infrastructure that could then be wired for recessed lighting and a much-coveted sound system. As convincing as my aesthetic reasoning might have been, I believe the sound system was what finally convinced my client to indulge this part of the project. In the end, coffering the ceiling made a significant impact. It enabled the addition of roughly 1 foot to the existing 8-foot ceiling in the most important space in the house.

AN ANTIQUE
MANTEL ADDS
CHARM IN AN
ECLECTIC LIVING
SPACE. LARGE
MILLED DOORS CAN
BE USED TO HIDE
OTHERWISE
EXPOSED
BOOKSHELVES
PRONE TO CLUTTER.

A FORMER
STORAGE
OUTBUILDING
WAS
CONVERTED
TO A LOFT
SUMMER
STUDIO. AN
UNTITLED DREW
SHIFLETT
SCULPTURE SITS
ON THE COFFEE
TABLE.

While refining a space with architectural detail can greatly enhance its appeal, once again don't overlook the obvious, that being the very use of the space. One of my more challenging projects led me to reconsider the traditional dining room. The home owner did not often use the awkwardly shaped dining area, the product of a former renovation. A bar area had been carved out of the original larger dining room. The bar area was very attractive, with significant millwork, but it was difficult for guests to navigate around it when the dining table was fully extended for a large sit-down dinner. Since the family was more likely to hold intimate gatherings, the solution was to figure out how to gracefully integrate the charming bar area rather than remove it.

Ideally suited for a convertible use consistent with the family's lifestyle, this space would serve better as a library than a dining room for its principal use. To accommodate this dual purpose, we added a column on either side of the area between the dining space/library and the bar. These columns projected slightly from the wall and delineated the bar area, whereas the addition of a doorway would have been too confining. Due to the age of the house, it was important that reclaimed antique columns be used in lieu of newly manufactured reproductions. I was fortunate to locate two nineteenth-century wooden columns that effectively separated the dining/library and bar areas while optically suggesting that the room was rectangular, consistent with the fully extended dining table.

Without its leaves, the table seated four, with the capacity to seat twelve on the rare occasion that this would be required. It was critical that the table have adequate heft in its smallest state to carry what was still a relatively large room. This was achieved by designing the table with a significant apron and columnar base. Finish was also a concern. A dark finish was chosen to add visual weight to this very focal table.

Wing chairs were appropriate both in the context of the library and as head chairs when the table was fully expanded for dining. Finally, we surrounded the space with bookshelves, lending intimacy without any appreciable loss of usable space. (Remember, bookshelves can be as shallow as 11 inches.) A once relatively dormant room is now routinely used by the entire family.

the nucleus of the home

Aesthetics should be carefully considered with the kitchen. It is, after all, the heart of most homes. And on a practical space-planning level, interaction between the chef and family or guests becomes critical. In spite of the fact that the kitchen is a known congregation area, acoustics are sometimes overlooked, which can defeat the comfort of the space. When choosing finishes as design elements, an attractive way to insulate sound is through the use of softer options that would be more likely thought of for elsewhere in the home. Depending on the traffic, wood floors can add architectural interest while absorbing sound. Ceiling treatments present a great opportunity for enhancing the beauty and acoustical function of the kitchen. Once again, consider how you might use traditional materials in nontraditional ways. Bead board, which is usually associated with cottage style, can be appropriately used in an urban setting as well.

In one home, I used large expanses of bead board in a chevron pattern on a ceiling bisected by beams that formed quadrants, creating a modern ceiling treatment with a subtle suggestion of texture.

Consider mounting your kitchen cabinets to the ceiling. This will provide more storage and visually suggest cleaner lines and a more generous sense of space. Generally the space left between the top of a cabinet and the ceiling is wasted, accumulating clutter and dust even under the best care.

KITCHEN SHELVING
IS FASHIONED
AFTER AN ITALIAN
ETAGERE.

windows

Beware the dreaded picture window, which tends to have a substantial visual presence; it touches neither the floor nor the ceiling and is generally placed at the wall's center in lieu of a perfectly good piece of art. Perhaps this is the origin of its namesake? I once addressed this challenge in a condominium setting. Community bylaw prohibitions were such that a picture window could not be changed from the exterior of the building; therefore a clever interior remedy was called for. Both walls flanking the window were built out as floor-to-ceiling bookcases, creating a recess at the window. Full-height shutters were placed at the window, suggesting that the window ran from the floor to the ceiling. These louvered shutters obstructed an otherwise unattractive view while allowing diffused light into the space. Inside the niche, I placed a curvaceous camelback sofa. What had been an unusable space became a favorite spot for the home owner to recline with a good book.

With some persuasion, many of my clients have discovered that enhancing the envelope of a room not only improves the aesthetic and comfort but also enhances value. By the time we approach a second project together, the same clients who once protested cosmetic changes appear at meetings armed with clippings dedicated solely to architectural detail. "After all," they remind me, "it adds value."

the last word

The thoughtful addition of architectural detail will enhance your interior by providing a sense of light and space.

A VINTAGE
INDUSTRIAL
CEILING FAN.

ART CREATES
A VISUAL
PROCESSION
FROM ONE ROOM
TO THE NEXT.

4 blend

use continual color and space planning to achieve flow

Space planning is a critical part of designing a home. The objective, apart from the obvious orientation of furnishings in each room, is to create a natural flow from room to room and from the indoors out. A house has to unfold in a way that makes sense. Each room in the home should flow gracefully into the next. This is achieved through continuity of common elements—the more outstanding of which is wall color. An optimal objective is to make the walls disappear. I achieve this through careful gradation of similar colors that imperceptibly change as you progress through each room. Though they are discreet, if you were to compare the first room in the procession to the last, you would discover distinct color differences. Likewise, furniture choices and textile palettes should relate without appearing to be purposeful; only the slightest nuance is needed to unify the rooms in your home. Furniture placed throughout the home should also have a similar scale.

In planning, as in all aspects of the process of designing and decorating your home, I cannot overemphasize the importance of contemplating your lifestyle. A room that is beautiful in passing is not the goal. Rooms need to be welcoming. Honestly assess how you will use spaces most frequently. Orient furniture to create a sense of intimacy.

a harmonious blend

My goal in defining a home is to integrate elements that complement rather than compete. When creating a color palette, whether warm or cool, be consistent throughout.

To select paint, first determine whether you gravitate toward a warm or a cool palette. This is an essential commitment as it will later affect textile choices that may otherwise clash without adequate forethought. I tend toward warm colors—whites with earthen undertones such as olive, putty, khaki, cocoa, lichen, and umber. In the converse, a cool palette consists of colors with blue and gray undertones. In either case, consistency within the chosen family of paints and textiles will create calm in an environment. Consistent palettes disappear in contrast to the jarring boundaries created by random bold color transitions. Think of hue rather than color. There should be a continuity of palette. Wall colors can differ from room to room, but the hues should relate, so that the colors wash into each other.

To see this concretely, look at a color wheel and notice how the colors subtly graduate. Consider this as you approach paint color in your home. Similar hues are essential to harmonizing the rooms in your home, creating the illusion of more space, particularly where rooms offer a view or access to one another.

FURNITURE
ALSO CREATES
LOGIC WHERE
ROOMS MEET.

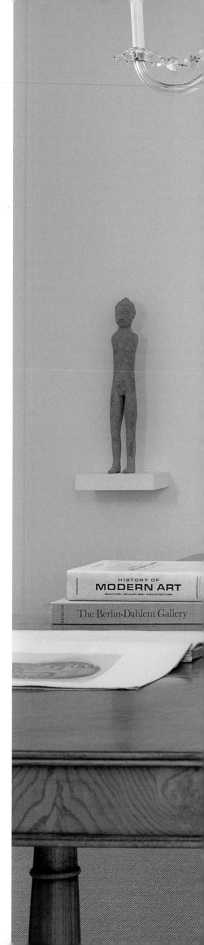

THE FOYER
FINISHES AND
COLOR PALETTE
GIVE WAY TO A
FAMILY GATHERING
AREA IN THE
DISTANCE.

A caveat: It is useful to see an actual sample of the paint on the walls where you intend to use it. It will invariably be different from the color wheel or chip, due to differing light exposure. The hue will also read differently at various times of the day. This applies in natural daylight as well as ambient or artificial light. Be sure to see the paint in all probable light scenarios.

Consider this when selecting trim color as well. Trim becomes more pronounced when it distinctly differs from the wall color. Dial the color slightly up or down a shade from the wall color to suggest depth and to discreetly emphasize the architecture.

subtle wall color and furnishings

I suggest a continual color palette throughout the home. The wall color becomes the backdrop for all other furnishings, and the home's logic must transcend all layers of design. To create continuity in one client's residence, for example, I had the living room walls painted a very pale yellow and used upholstered furnishings of primarily natural linens in a warm hue consistent with the walls. I added glazed jade garden stools in front of a fireplace, a subtle celadon ceramic lamp, and the faintest suggestion of lichen, green, and blue on a striated pillow. This living room led through two arched doorways to a sunroom, which was softly washed in a pale shade of sea foam. If you have a discreet color in a foreground, play off it by painting a distant room in that color. This is one way to maintain continuity. If each room transitions in the same hue, then color change does not mark the movement from one room to the next, which creates a greater sense of calm and space. The pale yellow of the formal living room and the pale sea foam of the sunroom were of the same color value and intensity. In this context, the procession of color creates depth and subsequently draws you into the next room.

THE EXTERIOR PAINT
BEGINS A SUBTLE
INTERPLAY OF COLOR
GRADATION
THROUGHOUT THE
INTERIOR ROOMS.

One of the most common mistakes I encounter in the home is abrupt color transition from one room to the next. This is a surprisingly common occurrence in the dining room. Perhaps people try more daring design treatments in their dining rooms because they aren't thought of as an everyday part of the home. Instead, maybe because dining rooms are typically used at night, home owners try to create a memorable atmosphere in which to entertain guests.

This treatment does not take into account the fact that this part of the home does carry visually in the ordinary course of a day. These rooms, as romantic as they may appear on occasion, can otherwise be a jarring departure from the rest of the home. Choose a color that is consistent with the palette throughout if you elect to treat any public room with a distinctly different color. For example, if most rooms in the house have a lighter hue, then use a hue of the same color, only slightly darker, for the space you want to distinguish.

The most common example of the dining room disconnect is the ubiquitous red-lacquered dining room. Red lacquer unto itself is beautiful in the proper setting, but usually not in a house that is otherwise neutral in palette. My preference would be for a more subtle backdrop, but in some cases, that's not an option. In one such instance, the red was non-negotiable since one partner was emphatic, so our solution was to neutralize the palette. To harmonize the dining room with adjacent rooms, which were all neutral, we used textiles of washed khaki, umber, and pale apricot on draperies, seat cushions, rugs, and interior cabinet backs. We backed the cabinets flanking a fireplace in a neutral grass cloth and placed terra-cotta decoratives in them, as the red lacquer had orange and russet undertones. I chose a rug with a natural background and the faintest presence of red to complement the walls. The natural raw silk drapery was banded with a deep sienna velvet. Dark wood Asian dining chairs were softened with seat pillows of wheat-colored woven wool that had the slightest hint of sienna. The adjacent foyer rug was carefully chosen to include colors that faintly suggested the dining room's palette while integrating color from neighboring rooms.

THE INTERIOR
AESTHETIC
SEAMLESSLY
INTEGRATES
FUNCTION.

DETERIORATED
ORIGINAL WOOD
FLOORING WAS
UPDATED WITH
LIMESTONE
HONORING THE
FORMER PATTERN.

floors and other key details

Rooms have to relate to one another in order to create a sense of welcome and procession. Floor finishes and rugs are essential to maintaining a cohesive flow. Including the floor and ceiling, any given room possesses six walls. People generally don't labor over floor finishes as they do wall color, but again, floors are just as important when looking at the space as a whole. Floors frame rugs in the same sense as art is framed; the choice of "matting" is critical. I often layer dark floors with natural sisal area rugs, topped by antique rugs. The dark floor frames the sisal, which offers a crisp contrast that modernizes the space. The antique rug should be a wash of color and pattern so it is not too pronounced or graphic (think watercolor), blending in quietly with the rest of the room. In turn, sisal frames antique rugs, removes their staid formality, and contemporizes them.

I frequently use rugs to guide wall-color selection, particularly when working with antique or found rugs. It's generally more challenging to work in the reverse. For paint selection, I often choose the least pronounced color in a rug—the hint of pale green represented by a leaf in a pattern, for instance.

Fireplace surrounds are another visually imposing element of a room that may go unnoticed but can have significant impact. They may take up a lot of visual space, which is why it's important to keep them simple. These should be treated consistently throughout the home. Plain light gray slate surrounds generally work beautifully in most contexts, modern or traditional, because they blend into the firebox. Paint fireboxes with fire-retardant black paint since they will darken with use in any event.

THE PRIMITIVE
GRECIAN URN
BECKONS
THROUGH THE
MEANDERING
HALLWAY.

elements of style

My love for old books extends beyond my enjoyment of reading them. I also collect them, and I recommend that my clients do the same. On a visual note, old books lend great character to a room and allow you to integrate discreet color into a space.

Flowers present another opportunity to introduce color. There's no need for large quantities of flowers in expensive vessels. Avoid anything arranged; a fragrant spray or a bud vase with a single flower will make an elegant statement. For bunches, use similar flowers rather than mixing different varieties and colors. Simple gestures can thoughtfully humanize a space.

choose multifunction furniture

Be sure to select furniture that can serve multiple uses. This bit of logic probably arose for me out of economic necessity as I was buying my first furniture pieces. One sure way to rationalize the purchase of something you may otherwise think of as frivolous or extravagant is to assign it many uses. Case in point: my ambitious purchase of a nineteenth-century mahogany wine table—otherwise known as a gentleman's social table. Cleverly designed in the shape of a hollowed semicircle, it was intended as a bar of sorts by its original design. It also serves beautifully as a writing desk that can float at a room's center due to its form, being attractive from all vantages. This continues to be one of my favorite pieces, and while it routinely sits in front of a fireplace in my master bedroom, it has also served well as a bar or a graceful foyer piece to hold a guest book when I've had larger gatherings.

If you are just beginning to furnish your home, the good news is that you can forecast a clear logic that will later allow you to freely move furniture from room to room. This is one more reason to choose classic forms and neutral

ARCHITECTURAL
TREE HULLS
SERVE AS
SCULPTURAL
SCREENS.

textiles. As your taste evolves, or if a move is in your future, a chair that was once appropriate in the living room may later be placed in the bedroom. The idea is that over time, your furnishings should have a consistency that will allow them to travel about the home and not be confined to one particular space.

A decorative screen is a staple piece given its multipurpose uses. It can block a doorway to maintain some element of surprise when you're hosting a party, for instance, while adding texture and depth to a room. A screen can offer utility while reading either as art or architecture. In effect, a screen is a moving wall.

creating a sense of intimacy

A recurring challenge in space planning is creating a sense of intimacy, particularly in large spaces. An immediate antidote for this is floating all primary seating at the center of the room. This encourages greater communion than furniture placed at the perimeter of a room, which invariably creates a void at the room's center. In the traditional context, the typical living room comes in two varieties—the rectangle or the square. Although there seems to be an overwhelming instinct to line the edges of a room with furniture, it's important to think outside the box, or, in this case, outside the center of the box.

In my own rectangular living room, a monumental fireplace and mantel topped with a large antique mirror dominate one end. The opposing side is balanced with a large abstract canvas on the wall and an antique grand piano that projects into the center of the room. These two walls carry a similar visual weight. I center the space with two camelback sofas that lend curve to the linear

WHITE PORCH
PAINT UNIFIES ODD
WOOD FLOORING.

architecture of the room. A vintage rug rests atop a larger sisal rug. Diminutive antique chairs line the room as functional sculpture; they are easily moved for conversation in larger groups. A small bench doesn't have any real visual consequence, yet you can pull it up for a close conversation. Benches prove especially handy for hosts, who can offer the comfort of seating to their guests in a gesture of hospitality. There's something casual and intimate about benches even in a very formal setting.

Another way to give a more human scale to a large living room is to place two sofas back-to-back in the center of the room. This particular arrangement bisects the room, creating the option of more intimate gatherings as it delineates two more separate seating areas at either sofa in a space that might otherwise be daunting. A large room can be unwelcoming if you have only a few guests. Sectioning off an area invites them to collect at one side. Create several intimate gathering areas in a single large room rather than accommodating a large space with large furniture.

Be cognizant of the seated guest's vantage point. Consider views, both interior and exterior. Orient seating to take advantage of the best sight lines. Thoughtful interior vignettes should also allow for seeing into adjacent rooms and hallways.

longevity

Beware of trends. Choose classic patterns and colors for drapery and upholstery textiles. A contemporary pattern may date a space in short order. Turn to fashion for advice and reference. The navy blazer and the black dress will no doubt outlive the bold impulse purchases that have found their way to the back of the closet.

Subtle textile palettes throughout the home support the sense of continuity as rooms unveil themselves. Avoid dark upholstery, especially on large pieces of furniture. Punches of dark color or pattern should be used sparingly; otherwise they may become too present, defeating the cohesive blending that is the objective. If you want to incorporate bolder choices, limit them to smaller pieces, such as footstools, an upholstered seat on a bench, or a pillow. If you find an oversize windowpane pattern or a citrus shade you like, use these on pillows rather than on a sofa, chair, or ottoman. If you have a penchant for marigold, select a soft shade of yellow rather than a bold one. You'll be comfortable living with these longer than you will with a more of-the-moment selection.

Careful selection of textiles will serve you well in the future because you may wish to move things from one room to another over time. Given the investment, anticipate possible reuse of furniture pieces as lifestyles change and kids go off to college. I encourage the use of classic forms and discreet colors and patterns. Upholstery fabric with a lighter hand may produce a more tailored outcome, accentuating form and graceful lines. When using pattern, choose time-honored classics, such as faint glen plaids, herringbones, or muted toiles. These have longevity and are far less likely to date over the years.

Elements such as grand staircases, huge bejeweled chandeliers, and trendy paint colors inevitably date a space. As tempting as it may be to add embellishment, if given an option, it's always wiser to go with the more understated.

the last word

Remember to plan your home so that rooms function individually while contributing to the overall sense of flow in the collective. This will produce a sense of calm throughout your home.

WALLPAPER TRANSITIONS INTO DISTANT EXTERIOR FOLIAGE.

A VINTAGE
LIBRARY CHAIR
IN ORIGINAL
TOBACCO
LEATHER.

5 touch

choose inviting textures and timeworn textiles

To create a welcoming environment, choose textiles that are soft to the touch in muted, understated colors and patterns. Use the same principles here as you did in the selection of wall colors.

When using faint colors, you can highlight the subtle differences and create a sense of depth through the juxtaposition of various textures. Be aware that certain fabrics are more welcoming than others. Generally speaking, we've come a long way from the plastic slipcover, but as old habits die hard, there still seems to be some penchant for "off-limits" living rooms. Somehow, these presumed-to-be formal spaces are inevitably treated with formal regalia. Think of living rooms you've seen decorated with silks, satins, damasks, and moirés.

A NAPOLÉON ARMCHAIR
RE-COVERED IN LICHEN
VELVET WITH ORIGINAL
SILK STRIPE BLENDS
WITH A TIMEWORN RUG
LAID ON THE REVERSE.

These textiles say no kids, no pets—only the most coordinated adults are welcome. They suggest perfectly upright posture and no spilling. While I appreciate the opulence of these fabrics in the appropriate environment, most often they do not suit everyday wear and tend to be unwelcoming and uncomfortable. Conversely, matte textiles suggest more approachable, comfortable environments. Instead of upholstering furniture with unduly fancy textiles, use linens, cottons, velvets, suedes, and other fabrics that are soft to the touch. Sometimes an environment can be so precious that it becomes uninviting. Subconsciously you don't want to sit down in these settings for fear that you may disrupt them.

I encourage making rooms that suggest use. You can execute a beautiful, welcoming space with approachable textiles. Fill sofa cushions with down feathers rather than foam. Down-feather cushions leave impressions after someone sits on them instead of stiffly springing back. While some might fluff cushions before guests arrive, I'm inclined to depress them to suggest that it's all right to have a seat. Choose soft, tactile fabrics that will become softer with wear, such as cotton velvets. Pair them with linens, chenilles, suedes, woven cottons, or woolens. Billiard cloth has a sensuous hand similar to that of cashmere. I have covered bed pillows in sheared terry cloth at an ocean retreat. Even in a monotone palette, these textiles create depth and contrast. Linen upholstery always lends a casual crispness to a space. In fact, you can make the most traditional chair modern if you cover it in a neutral linen. One of my prize finds was a chair hidden under a quilted floral when I bought it at an antiques shop. It was an eyesore. Once it was reupholstered in a simple linen, a striking, sculptural form was unveiled.

A RUG MAY BE
MORE APPEALING
PLACED ON ITS
TIMEWORN UNDERSIDE.

One way to subtly introduce patterns is to use patterned textiles on the reverse side. An active pattern can take on a timeworn character in this execution. This is a particularly good compromise if you're on the fence about incorporating pattern, since this treatment can be safer, offering greater longevity. As with the continual palette suggested for wall colors, the effect is that of a quiet watercolor; the pattern should read as barely discernible shadows. This technique is effective with draperies, tapestries, pillows, and rugs.

Rugs are challenging because they can visually consume a room. The rug should marry into the environment. I often use antique or very worn vintage handwoven rugs on the reverse. The older vegetable-dyed rugs seem to serve best for this purpose. The colors and patterns of new, machine-made rugs can be too graphic. Old rugs that have been walked upon for years are preferable. The wear mutes color and suggests options for integrating those same faint colors into the neutral textile palette. When you are integrating color from the rug into the textile palette, choose one of the colors from the rug that is least pronounced. As I suggested in chapter 4, if the rug has slight hints of pale green, use a similar saturated green velvet on a pillow when you wish to add more colorful contrast to a space; alternatively, match the subdued green in the rug.

Area rugs can make or break a space. The rug should not be the focal point. As with textiles, avoid complicated graphics with finite patterns and vibrant colors. These can overwhelm a room and present major challenges when you are selecting fabrics. A rug with a large center medallion may compromise furniture placement as it suggests that all furniture pieces reference the graphic as a guide for placement, and it may cause the furniture to appear off center in relation to the medallion. Look for rugs with movement throughout, where pattern is discreet both in the body and the border so that it does not inadvertently confine furniture placement by framing it. In general, you'll want to place rugs that have a similar density, wear, and composition throughout your home for continuity. Flatweaves and low-pile handwovens in muted shades quietly blend in any setting. As with abrupt color change, a rug can be jarring if inconsistent, even in a distant room. Select rugs of similar character so that if you move furniture from one space to another, you'll have more than one option for placement. This is why you might want to find your rugs first.

TOILE USED ON THE
REVERSE UNIFIES
THE CONTRASTING
DARK WOODS AND
LIGHT ENVELOPE.

A MULBERRY
LINEN SEAT
WASHES INTO
THE WAINSCOT.

upholstery options

I chuckle at some of the would-be land mines I negotiate between a client's tolerance and certain nonnegotiable aesthetic principles. There is, for example, a standing debate between the skirt and leg proponents. Many believe that a fully upholstered piece of furniture, skirted to the floor, is more comfortable. Remember, the skirt's primary function most often is to hide the legs without affecting comfort. It's the construction of the seat and back that adds comfort. A room filled only with fully upholstered furniture pieces may quickly seem crowded. Sofas on legs, particularly when floated in a room's center, consume far less visual mass. When these are coupled with properly scaled, fully upholstered chairs, a room will have a greater sense of space than it would if filled with a suite of heavy-looking matching upholstered furniture. On the other hand, there are drawbacks to having too many legs showing on sofas and chairs in a single room. This can create a sense of rigid formality. If the furniture in a room is too leg heavy, add a skirt or a slipcover on a chair or two to add visual play.

Just as horizontal stripes are unflattering on certain body types, a large piece of furniture such as a sofa shouldn't be covered in a bold print. Graceful architecture, particularly on larger principal pieces in a room, is accentuated when executed in a subtle fabric. Camelback sofas can have an extraordinary grace of line, particularly the early examples. An overscale sofa may be more gracefully reinterpreted through the use of fewer seat cushions, replacing three individual cushions with one longer down-filled cushion. On that note, for vintage pieces that need upholstering, minor alterations to enhance visual appeal may be in fact a sound investment, even with the cost of alteration.

SUMPTUOUS KID
LEATHER WITH
CHENILLE INVITES
A GOOD READ.
BEHIND IT, A HEAVY
LINEN DRAPE IS
BANDED WITH DARK
OATMEAL VELVET.

As you begin your search for that perfect sofa, keep an eye out for graceful curving and appealing lines on the profile. I look for mixed mediums—upholstered pieces with wood detail, for example. Look for those with a low profile. Placing these in a room will preserve visual sight lines and allow you to add more furniture, and such pieces are less likely to create barriers within a room. Conversely, higher-profile furniture pieces can be cumbersome.

pairing textiles: opposites attract

The interplay of masculine and feminine elements in a room can add interesting contrast. For example, in the construction of a drape, mix a nubby burlap body with a sumptuous cotton velvet band. Or place an upholstered cube in kidskin leather on top of a timeworn rug. Sometimes I keep a distance between the two. For instance, I might upholster a sofa in cotton toile on the reverse in a room with burlap drapery. Mix fabrics just as you do modern furniture with antiques.

Climate, geography, architecture, and lifestyle should all be contemplated when deciding which textiles to use. Linen is one of my favorite textiles. It accommodates very tailored upholstery and hangs beautifully as a drape. It suggests a carefree, organic environment and, what's more, it has a unifying neutrality. Depending upon its density it can be appropriate in most climates throughout the year. All of this said, it wrinkles, which may altogether exclude it as a choice for those who cannot tolerate this characteristic. If you can, it is an excellent option.

Do not choose a textile that you cannot live with. This is of particular note when working with a design consultant. If you are averse to the feel of a particular fabric, persist in finding another selection. A textile may be beautiful, but

A BED INSPIRED
BY AN EARLY
FORM IS MODERN
IN ITS FINISH AND
WITH ITS NATURAL
LINEN DUVET.

there's no point in selecting it if you won't live comfortably with it. In fact, given the proliferation of credible synthetics, rather than a delicate, high-maintenance fabric, you may prefer something stain- and water-resistant.

Lifestyle should be considered when selecting textiles. Fabric choices will dictate the level of comfort or formality in a home appropriate to your lifestyle, so approach these decisions with care.

One of my most memorable projects speaks directly to this point. Shortly after completing a city residence for clients, I was asked to work on a property they had purchased in the country. I was thrilled to work with them again as we had such a shared aesthetic. When I finally went to visit the property, however, my clients were struck by my response. Instantly, I knew this house would be treated outside of their expected aesthetic. When I walked into the house, I visualized myself reading a book under a blanket by a fire. This is what inspired the project and the critical selection of textiles that would honor the feeling of the house.

As collectors, the couple was partial to austere environments respectful of their fine art. The setting in the country called for more interactive textiles consistent with a sense of comfort and place. Here I promoted warm washes of colors on the walls with a tea-stained floral pattern and drapery that bled into the foliage outside the window. Generally, I think drapes should blend into either the walls or the nature beyond. Textile selections for upholstered pieces in this home were an appropriate departure, given the casual environment. My clients were willing to abandon the crisp linens of the city for enveloping chenilles, velvets, mohairs, and heavy burlaps.

A rural setting may require an altogether different approach from an urban one depending on the age or personality of the home owner. In one instance an extraordinary collection of antiques somehow needed to be contemporized.

Another couple had a number of family heirlooms that had been handed down through several generations. There were so many extraordinary antiques; each beautiful standing alone, together they suggested a formality inconsistent with the couple's lifestyle.

BOOKSHELVES
BACKED IN
GRASS-CLOTH
WALLCOVER
SUBTLY WARM
THE SPACE.

It is not uncommon that heirloom pieces are in need of modernization. At the risk of offending purists, one way to address this is by reinventing them with a contemporary textile. An upholstered slipper chair is a perfect example: It can be innocuous in linen in a modern setting or it can take an absolutely traditional posture in a traditional environment when dressed in an active floral. Once again, logic will prevail. In the city, you may want more formality, whereas in the country a more relaxed environment is called for.

In this case, I reupholstered the antiques in contemporary textiles (by this I mean modern relative to the expected period treatment). The pale sage palette throughout the house—on the walls and floors—accentuated the architecture of the upholstered furniture and created a calm backdrop, respectful of the sculptural antiques. Paring down the art collection and placing the pieces throughout the home made each one that much more interesting and important.

One not-so-obvious venue where the integration of textiles helped harmonize two spaces was in adjoining his and hers dressing rooms in another couple's home. Contrast of color and texture was once again a logical place to start. The spaces had to accommodate a number of specific functions, yet because they were contiguous, they still needed to relate to one another. Not surprisingly, they also needed to be distinctly different—men's club meets day spa. The first challenge was to choose base colors that would work in both areas. Pale gray and Pommery mustard were neutral enough, and could be dialed up or down to suit the spaces appropriately. His walls were upholstered in gray flannel with a Pommery ticking stripe lining all glass cabinets, drawers, and interior closets. Hers were upholstered in a faint floral pattern on the reverse. The field was cream with vines and flowers in gray and Pommery. The interior linings of the cabinets and drawers were the same ticking stripe. Each space worked beautifully alone and thoughtfully with the other.

the last word

Create a welcoming environment with calm textiles in soothing, understated colors and patterns.

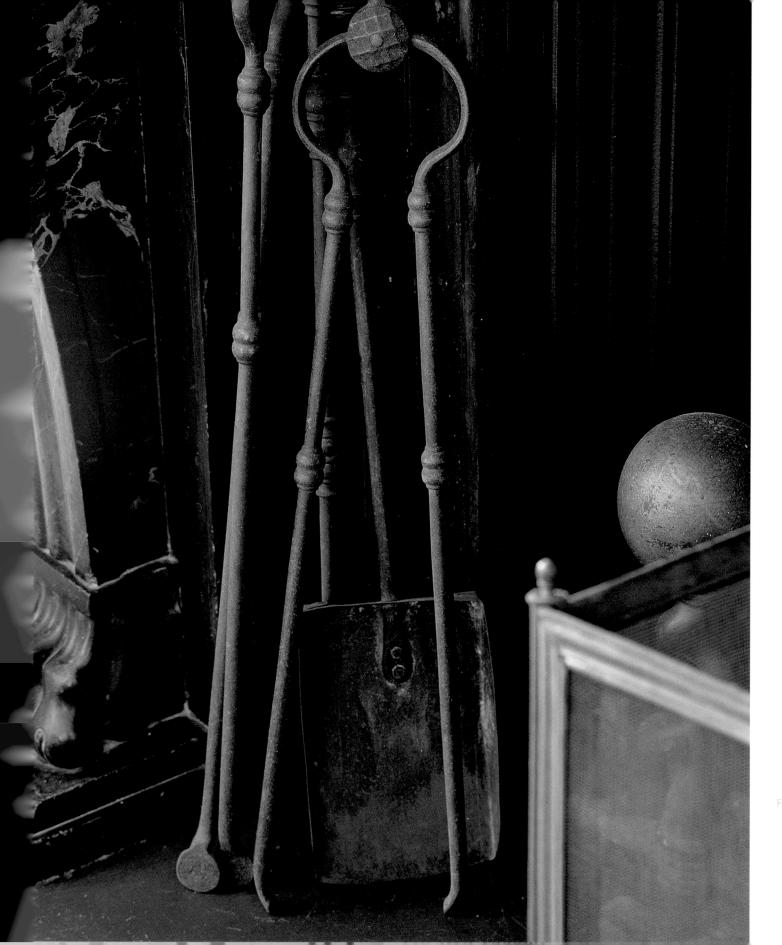

TIMEWORN
FIREPLACE TOOLS
AND A SCREEN
SUGGEST
BYGONE FIRES.

A DIMINUTIVE
HARPSICHORD IS
AN ALTERNATIVE
TO A GRAND
PIANO.

using furniture that is more in keeping with the human scale. Many people mistakenly presume pared-down furniture compromises comfort. This is not necessarily so: Comfort depends on variables such as slope of back and fill of seat. Scale is where things can go haywire. Many different kinds of furnishings can live together if they are of a similar scale.

don't tip the scale

Scale is just one element that helps establish balance in a room. If one object in a room overwhelms either on its own or by its placement, this may significantly compromise both functional and visual comfort within the space. A room can visually tip over if too many heavy objects are placed at one end. Some sofas are absurdly long; some can be ridiculously deep. Sitting and sinking are two different things. Once you get in, you ought to be able to get out. It is not uncommon to find sofa arms so exaggerated in size that they displace would-be seating on the sofa. Overscale arms may seem more comfortable at first glance, but functionally they do not serve any better than a more pared-down arm. Look for classically scaled proportions on contemporary sofas and chairs. The objective is generally to sit comfortably with good posture. An 18-inch curve to the arm does not assist in this goal. Overscale furniture in an urban context can be even more challenging. I've heard more than one tale of a sofa that would not fit through a front door, much less into an elevator.

A NINETEENTH-CENTURY ARMOIRE MAKES A BOLD STATEMENT NEXT TO A GRECIAN VESSEL IN THIS SPARE SETTING.

PERIOD ASIAN
SCREENS CREATE
SYMMETRY AND
CONCEAL CHINA
STORAGE CLOSETS.

THE DARK MANTEL
AND THE ASIAN
ALTAR TABLE IN
THE FOREGROUND
BALANCE THE
ROOM.

plain geometry

I have found that it helps to study the geometric relationships between the space and the furniture to be placed. In a linear environment, be sure to integrate subtle curves as you select your furnishings. A graceful camelback sofa, a bergère with a curved seat, a side chair with an oval spider back, the arc of a baby grand, an oval back on a wall sconce—all soften a linear space. You can balance a room by sensitivity to these opportunities.

The dining room presents a challenge. As mentioned, it can fast take on the feeling of a boardroom with its chairs rigidly standing at attention around a table. The shape of your dining room will influence the shape of the table you choose. If you have a rectangular dining room, a rectangular table is generally called for unless the room can hold two round tables. If you have a square dining room, a round table will allow for a more intimate gathering. Of course proportion plays a critical role here. The table dimension should accommodate your particular needs. Round tables are inherently more egalitarian as

A GRACEFUL
MAHOGANY
BANISTER IS
SUPPORTED BY
SIMPLE IRON
PICKETS.

there is no head of the table. This is why I prefer them. Finding an antique or vintage table is particularly challenging given the limited options available to suit a particular space.

You can finesse the integration of antiques by pairing them with more diminutive contemporary pieces. This approach is also more accommodating of eclectic aesthetics, which call for an assortment of furniture styles. Antique Swedish chairs can be placed opposite an antique American table. Contemporary chairs might dwarf the same table. Though I have a penchant for antiques, I strive to maintain a modern sensibility. Antique doesn't preclude modern. One partner doesn't have to give up his antique collection because the other prefers Le Corbusier. It's a matter of scale and balance. Earlier American furniture is lauded for its purity of line. This is consistent with a variety of midcentury modern pieces. These antique and modern pieces coexist effortlessly.

Some rooms that lack architectural features can take on character through heavily ornamented pieces in the company of simple furnishings. Picture a chinoiserie console; the intricate hand painting is the equivalent of an extraordinary piece of art on a bare wall. Another way to juxtapose the old and the new might be to place a large modern canvas over a highly carved antique console. The modern canvas can calm the antique. Try to maintain a disciplined scale and ornament so that the hunt for the right objects and furniture is purposeful.

Balance should be contemplated not only in terms of the furniture but also in terms of the space itself. In some cases, partitions or fixed architectural elements can enhance depth and texture and rescue an otherwise impersonal envelope. For instance, a client had a typical loft— a cavernous rectilinear expanse with high ceilings, strong angles, and uninterrupted voids of space. The apartment needed to be humanized.

A GATELEG
LIBRARY TABLE
DEFINES THIS
DINING AND
READING ROOM.

A monumental architectural corbel was hung on the wall to serve as a console, which added texture, curve, and function to an otherwise monotonous expanse of wall. And the corbel's age added an unexpected layer to the clean, modern space.

Another client needed help managing the scale of a rather large penthouse so that the space would feel more approachable. In this case, we installed a large, antique leather screen in the living room, instantly rendering the space more intimate.

While a single significant piece appropriately placed can redefine a space, you have to be selective when you choose that piece. It is not uncommon to encounter a grand piano as an obligatory "statement" or "filler" in a large living room. As objects, pianos can be stunningly beautiful, particularly the antique variety. But a piano with a pronounced finish or ornamental finish does not discreetly blend into any environment. Depending upon the space and the piano, any composition can become as clichéd as the round center hall table in the curve of the center hall stair.

If you walk into a room and the piano is the first and only thing that draws your eye, then unless you play and/or it is an heirloom, a floating altar table or library table piled with books can produce the same impact, and may also serve as an alternative dining venue. If the piano isn't played, but rather is thought of more as sculpture, then consider an antique with a patinated veneer. Another alternative is the harpsichord. These tend to

VINING ENVELOPS THIS GARDEN. BALANCE IS ACHIEVED THROUGH ARCHITECTURAL SYMMETRY AND THOUGHTFUL FURNISHINGS.

be as interesting as objects, but more diminutive in scale and therefore less likely to overwhelm a room.

Rather than tempering the large scale of a space, many face an opposite challenge: They want smaller rooms to feel more spacious. Scale, function, and lifestyle should be carefully thought through when selecting furniture for this purpose. Clients who live in a charming town house wanted to make more intelligent use of the existing layout. The house was one of the more livable and engaging I have come across, but somehow it wasn't functioning as well as it could for their needs. Instead of physically altering the rooms, I combined the dining room, family room, and library functions into a single space. A round table was placed at the room's center, flanked by two antique tavern benches with a highly carved antique overhead chandelier. Bookshelves and cabinets were added on either side of the fireplace to hold china and the couple's favorite books.

In order to achieve balance, no one object or furniture piece should dominate a space. A piece that has great presence may, however, be called for. The point is to thoughtfully honor the way that you live in your own home.

the last word

Pay attention to your instincts when it comes to balancing a room. If a space feels impersonal or unwelcoming, sometimes adding a single interesting piece can impart approachability.

A METAMORPHIC
SETTEE ADDS
SEATING TO A
KITCHEN ALCOVE.

7 edit

select appropriate furniture
(less is more)

Design with bold strokes using a few well-chosen pieces of furniture and art. If every inch of a room is covered with wallpaper, draperies, tassels, and other furnishings, single objects lose their interest and importance. Spare environments are challenging as they are less visually forgiving and lack superfluous distractions. You must be particular and confident in your choices.

When buying furniture, be thoughtful and disciplined. Choose fewer pieces of greater quality and interest. You should first go looking, not shopping. If something flirts with you, trust that you will later find something that seduces you; discover what uniformly appeals to you before making any purchases. While an object or a furniture

piece may be beautiful standing alone, imagine it keeping company with other furniture pieces as you see the room evolving. You will discover that certain styles or periods appeal to you. When I began to furnish my first home, I noticed that I gravitated toward metamorphic campaign furniture. The golden age of travel in the nineteenth century inspired a genre of furniture and implements that had multiple uses, from trunks that became writing desks to four-poster beds that could be folded into a self-contained traveling case. One of my early purchases was a farm table that converts into a bench by the removal of four simple dowels. These early functional designs inspired several metamorphic pieces in my furniture collection. One piece was born of functional evolution. Just as I imagine inconvenience inspired early campaign design, discomfort while watching television was my muse. The sofa in my sitting room was too short to recline on. But the design so suited the space that I had it rebuilt so that one arm would fold down, allowing me to comfortably recline.

As you're shopping, you may find single pieces that serve many space-saving needs. A demilune drop-leaf game table could be placed against a wall with a lamp and a great piece of art, or it could be combined with a second demilune table to form an intimate dining table between two opposing settees. Don't limit your invention to simple functionality. Experiment with combinations of different periods and wood species. Try whitewashed chairs with a dark table or modern chairs with an antique table. Put a modern Tizio lamp on an antique table. Part of creating interesting and unique environments is juxtaposing furniture pieces and objects that have no obvious relationship to one another but that simultaneously counterbalance one another. If you own a desk made of a distinctive dark wood, perhaps you should look for a book cabinet veneered in a lighter wood with the faintest dark marquetry detail similar in color to the desk. This is a simple way to incorporate furniture pieces that might not otherwise be placed together. Additionally, on a space-saving note, this is less deliberate than placing several furniture pieces together with the obvious intention of matching them. Making furniture choices anticipating the future mixing of pieces makes purchases more thoughtful so that fewer pieces may better serve. There should be a subtle nexus between pieces, most critically scale. Classic shapes and timeless design hidden under unappealing upholstery or wood can be given new life with a good polishing or coat of paint.

chairs

As you search for principal pieces, do not overlook the importance of chairs. A graceful wing chair can help define an entire room. Examples from the Federal period are particularly appealing because their forms can be so brilliantly simple. I find the modern counterpart, the Egg chair, equally appealing for its form and comfort. Though an Egg chair and a wing chair are generally thought to be at opposite ends of the design continuum, both are transitional and even interchangeable in the proper environment. One way to enhance the architecture of an earlier chair might be to remove the seat cushion and replace it with a thin down-filled pad. This makes the chair sit lower, so be sure that this alteration suits your comfort. You may find the resulting chair more enveloping. The original design intent of the wing chair, after all, was to cradle the sitter and protect him or her from drafts.

living room seating

Lately, it seems that living rooms are becoming more living spaces than bastions for formal entertaining, so real lifestyle considerations should be contemplated. If you only occasionally entertain large numbers of guests, you needn't decorate the room with a full complement of cumbersome chairs. Once again, benches hidden under side tables or coffee tables and attractive diminutive chairs can serve as discreet overflow seating. When you determine how you want to furnish the space, base your decision on how it will be used on a daily basis.

A client had a small living room that needed to function for both intimate and large gatherings. The central fireplace influenced the furniture placement. No matter what size the room is, there should be a distinctly intimate area somewhere within it. In this case, instead of placing the sofas across from each other, I placed one sofa in a bay window and another near an adjacent fireplace, with a large bench opposite the principal sofa. This way, guests could sit facing either the sofa in the bay window or the sofa near the fireplace. Here a bench provides flexibility for gatherings of a few friends or many.

THE PRACTICAL,
ONCE-COMMON
TEA-HEIGHT TABLE
PROVIDES EASE OF
REACH AND
LEGROOM.

dining room tables

A dining room table should rarely be surrounded by matching chairs. This invariably lands you in a conference room. A dining table is a substantial purchase and can serve multiple uses, so select your dining table with alternative uses in mind. If the table is antique or vintage, make sure that all the leaves are present and working; it could later break down to serve as a desk. Sit in a chair at various places around the table to ensure that the apron height and leg placement will feel comfortable for your guests. Try to avoid precious finishes. They may subconsciously create caution, which can frustrate comfortable dining.

coffee and tea tables

Try a tea-height table in front of your sofa rather than a typical coffee table. Tea-height tables work beautifully between opposing sofas because coffee tables that are too low may be awkward and occupy too much visual mass. When tables are higher, they may be more practical because of reach and legroom. If you have opposing sofas, be aware of your sight line, particularly with lower profile sofas. A table should not obstruct interaction. You want the table to be low enough that you can see the person across from you, but high enough that you can reach over and have a cup of tea comfortably. Leather or parchment Asian trunks also serve well as coffee tables, integrating beautifully into most environments. They can easily be elevated on a frame of metal legs, and they also provide discreet storage.

AN ANTIQUE HUNT
TABLE CAN FLOAT
IN A SPACE AND
SERVE AS A
WRITING DESK.

AN ANTIQUE
HEADBOARD AND
TESTERS ARE
MODIFIED TO
ACCOMMODATE A
CONTEMPORARY
MATTRESS.

bedside tables

When it comes to bedside tables, I suggest large ones that provide plenty of room for books, magazines, a clock, and a phone. A chair can also serve as an unusual bedside table, particularly where space is at a premium. An important consideration here is ease of reach. A principal bedroom is one of the more important rooms in the home given the time spent there, but somehow these spaces are often neglected, sacrificing charm for utility. A large, round, tripod table may serve you as well as a bedside chest of drawers. Consider options other than the usual.

four-poster beds

Beds are challenging by virtue of their size, which makes them the natural focal point in the room. Four-poster beds work in both small and large bedrooms. In a small bedroom, the bed requires architectural interest all the more. In a large room, a four-poster can make a space more intimate and welcoming by filling a significant void. You may be surprised to discover that a four-poster bed can occupy less visual mass than a bed with a simple headboard, particularly as they inch their way up to king proportions.

Some of the more interesting beds I've come across have been antiques. They are, however, often prohibitive due to their size, which is most often incompatible with available manufactured mattresses and bedcovers. Some of them, upon careful

examination, may be altered without compromising their visual integrity, unless of course you're dealing with a fine antique. Beds of simpler design are more easily adapted, while elaborate veneers can be challenging. Sometimes a new side rail may be all that is necessary. On a note of comfort, while beautiful, the antique bed may be best relegated to a guest room.

Often it is more cost-effective to add wood panels on both sides of a headboard, which is what I once did to expand a bed's width to a standard contemporary size rather than order a custom mattress. After enlarging the four-poster this way, since the original finials had been lost over the years, I used bun-foot-style legs for a sofa as finials on the bed. You can substitute newly made parts from a restoration catalog because the design generally incorporates a screw that is compatible for attaching them.

desks

As noted, furniture pieces should be viewed as investments rather than disposable items; even moderately priced furnishings have become relatively expensive, so you should take care when purchasing them. Though it is hard to forecast one's future circumstances, it is prudent to try to envision where the piece might be used later, or how it might be adapted. For instance, a desk bought for its utility might have been a charming addition to a guest room had it been more thoughtfully chosen for its aesthetic qualities as well. Search for interesting pieces rather than a generic metal desk.

PATINATED
DRAWER FRONTS
DISPLAY DELICATE
HARDWARE.

Future adaptation is another way of valuing a purchase. An armoire bought for additional closet space in an apartment could later be retrofitted to house a home office or to hide a television. How this object may later be used may be dictated by how thoughtful you were when making the purchase. A recurring consideration is the home office. A beautiful desk or an antique armoire that later finds its way into a functional home office may make the office feel less disconnected from the furniture vocabulary of the rest of the house. Try not to place a desk against a wall; rather, float it in front of the wall so that when seated at the desk you're facing the room. This opens up the space.

the last word

Choose distinctive furnishings with care and confidence and they will serve you for years to come in varying locations as your home evolves.

AS DO ANTIQUES,
SIMPLE FORMS
WITHSTAND THE
TEST OF TIME.

THE ORIGINAL
MANTEL WAS
PRESERVED BY
PLACING IT ABOVE
THE NEW MANTEL
AND ADDING A
LOOKING GLASS.

8 reinvent

look beyond the obvious

One of the ways that an environment may be distinguished is by the creative use of objects intended for other purposes. This way of approaching antiques inspires much more inventive shopping. It is important to see beyond the obvious. An unlikely universe of objects may serve your intended need if you keep an open mind. This approach holds true as you search for items of broad utility, ranging from towel storage to something as simple as a collection of interesting vessels that attractively conceal toiletries. When shopping, be thorough. I have found clever alternatives for the mundane. Rather than buying a common soap dish for a powder room, look for a charming antique saucer that could serve this same purpose.

Furniture pieces can innovatively replace traditional cabinets and storage throughout the home. In my own bathroom I was challenged by the need to add interest to a very ordinary space. My immediate instinct was to integrate furniture into the space to add warmth to what so often becomes an austere echo chamber. I was challenged by two large bare walls, only one of which would accommodate a vanity due to existing plumbing conditions; the other would have to accommodate much-needed storage. I have to say my experience has been uncanny in that when I discover a specific need, the prayed-for object often reveals itself relatively shortly. This was the case when I was addressing my storage challenge in this bathroom. I was shopping in a remote countryside warehouse that had obviously taken advantage of a government building auction, given the vast stock of 1950s metal desks, file cabinets, and the like. Never disregard venues such as a liquidation warehouse. Some of my best finds have been in the recesses of these types of facilities. Look for auction postings and estate sales as well. You may find an interesting if not useful object. In this case, I found rows and rows of modular, glass-front oak barrister cabinets. The finish was not appealing, but I thought, "What an interesting and practical way to store towels." After I had them refinished, they made very attractive and functional storage.

A BARRISTER'S CABINET OFFERS ALTERNATIVE STORAGE IN A BATHROOM.

One of the advantages of refinishing something is that you may do the same with other objects that it might keep company with. The vanity I finally chose for this same bathroom was a former farm table, once again handicapped by finish and short legs. The barrister cabinet and the farm table were an unlikely pair, but they made sense once contemporized with an espresso brown varnish. I added marine veneer to the vanity to protect it from water spots. I addressed the height challenge by adding simple block feet that were slightly wider than the existing legs and were consistent with the piece's primitive quality. Because I had preordered enamel undermounting sinks and the accompanying hardware, the addition of sink holes to the table necessitated a carpenter with an exacting hand. A furniture piece adapted as a vanity is also an attractive solution in a small space such as a powder room. These can generally be readily adapted from small hall pieces that are traditionally placed against, or attached to, walls. Furniture pieces that are either rectangular or semicircular and elevated on legs are easily adapted. A substantial apron is also something to look for, so that the sink, once mounted, is concealed. While these parameters may seem a bit stifling, you'll be surprised by how often you come across these forms. The available variety ranges from simple to ornate. As positive as my experience has been finding these pieces, deadline constraints once forced me to consider a manufactured sink in a farmhouse bath project. Just as I was about to place it, I happened upon the most charming primitive demilune table, which was the perfect finish for the space. Don't give up.

A PRIMITIVE DEMILUNE CONSOLE WAS CONVERTED TO A VANITY. A RECTANGULAR MIRROR IS SUSPENDED BETWEEN TWO WINDOWS.

A STAIRWELL ONCE HIDDEN BY A WALL
BECOMES A SCULPTURAL FOCAL POINT
WHERE THREE ROOMS HAVE BECOME
ONE. THIS REQUIRES THE CAREFUL
INTEGRATION OF FURNITURE PIECES AND
THEIR FUNCTIONS.

functional revitalization

Don't be defeated by awkward space requirements. This is the true bastion of thoughtful reuse. Once again, in my own home I was challenged by a breakfast area that had been culled out of an existing kitchen, creating a relatively narrow solarium. In order to encourage intimate dining, this space was narrow by design. The future table would have to be purchased prior to the construction of a wall of French doors, as a table of the length I had in mind would not clear the entry. The table needed to be 119 inches long and no more than 28 inches wide to accommodate seating for twelve and room for door swing considerations. During a shopping trip I came across a table of almost precisely these dimensions. This good fortune was enhanced by the discovery that the table top pivoted into a bench, so that it could be easily maneuvered into the space post construction.

This situation highlights the need for thoughtful space planning. The table's dimensions affected the sizes of the future furniture pieces that would also be needed for the space to properly function. This was the equivalent of a self-imposed search for a needle in a haystack. My wish list was now confined to a maximum 14-inch-deep storage buffet that would provide ready access to napkins, cutlery, and the like. I found a nineteenth-century apothecary chest. Its multiple small drawers of varying sizes suited all of the small wares I needed access to. On the opposing wall, an antique baker's rack accommodates a collection of ironstone. Note that a two-sided baker's rack can serve as a partition in a small space. French doors separate the kitchen from the dining solarium, which is my preferred venue for casual entertaining; with the doors open, interaction between those sitting and those cooking adds to the intimacy and overall dining experience.

A METAMORPHIC CANDLEHOLDER IS CONVERTED INTO A WALL SCONCE.

adaptations

If you have limited options because of the pieces already in a room and are challenged to find a specific object to complete the space, keep an eye out for anything that might be altered to your needs. One of my favorite refuges is my studio, once a garage, in the country. The cement floor was retained, which defined the industrial character of the space. And because the space would open to the outdoors seasonally, I decided to use durable finishes. Oxidized metals were appropriate for the aesthetic as well. My studio was surprisingly simple to furnish, except for one focal piece: a large square, low coffee table for the room's center. I searched and searched to no avail until one day as I was leaving a shop, the vendor, with whom I shop routinely, said he had a garden piece that he thought I might like. At first glance I thought that this tall, awkward potting table, with its worn zinc top, was primitive even by my standards. Then it dawned on me to chop off the legs and preserve the 7-inch apron. The coffee table that I was searching for emerged from what started out as an entirely different piece of furniture.

A CHAIR MAKES
A CLEVER BEDSIDE
TABLE.

Proving that adaptive reuse extends beyond furniture and architecture to furnishings, I took two intricately carved corbels thought to be from the canopy of an eighteenth-century opium bed and suspended them from a wall in my foyer, where they support a limestone shelf. A Han dynasty figure is the focal object sitting atop this shelf. I wanted the foyer to be spare. The shelf carries a substantial wall. In order that the elaborate carving of the brackets did not overwhelm the space, they needed to stand alone.

Objects of a former life may serve contemporary utility, such as a pair of stone warmers to present cheeses and grapes or an old crab basket lined with table linens for apples or breads. An antique wool grain sack worn to softness serves as a throw. Overscale apothecary jars and rectangular clear glass containers, which were originally intended to hold battery acid, make for unique waste bins in a powder room. Early gas lamps can be adapted for modern use as electrified wall sconces. A beautiful marble mortar can make a handsome container for toiletries or soaps. A charred andiron with an attractive profile can add interest on a bookshelf as a sculpture. A cement vessel intended for plants might be used for kindling at fireside. Heavy crystal antique wine rinses might offer a perfect backdrop for soup, fruit, or ceviche on leaf lettuce; or, you could fill them with sorbet or with ice to chill a serving of caviar.

Antiquing in nearby Virginia offers so much potential for my reuse reveries. For example, some nineteenth-century Easter-egg molds would make a perfect container for small forks and appetizers. A vintage milk warmer would be ideal for pâté. A small antique shovel is certainly more interesting than your usual plastic dog-food scoop. A shallow, vintage washtub on wheels would make an unusual basin with a thick slab of Carrara marble as the surround. An 18-inch-deep nickel-and-Plexiglas display case with sliding doors, suspended upside down from a ceiling on tension wire above a counter, could look reminiscent of the plate storage

suspended over the counter in a vintage diner. Along this line of thinking, some objects that exist within the architecture of a home can be redefined. I once restored a diminutive pewter antique mantel in a historic home by placing it above a more substantial modern wood mantel I designed. I used the former antique mantel as a frame for an overmantel mirror.

When I was renovating my kitchen in the country, cabinets were lacking, and my completion date was looming. I didn't want to contend with a three-month lead time for custom cabinets. Instead I chose an antique three-door wooden pantry for alternative storage. This was cost-efficient and could be useful elsewhere later on. Furniture in a kitchen presents a viable alternative to a static row of cabinets that march down a wall. If you can find a piece of furniture that suits your needs and space, you may be better off integrating it. The reclaimed cupboard used in the kitchen of this cottage might work well in a bedroom in a future home. Look beyond the obvious as you select furniture and objects for your home.

the last word

When it comes to decorating, search for objects with unique character that can be used in unexpected ways throughout your home.

AN ANTIQUE
TELESCOPING
READING TABLE
ACCOMMODATES
ART DISPLAY.

9 study

shop for antiques with confidence

Introducing antiques to an environment adds character, a sense of story, and an acknowledgment of the past. When they are successfully mixed with modern pieces, there is no more attractive marriage. This can be daunting if unfamiliar territory, but do not let the process cause anxiety or intimidate you. An antique is simply something belonging to the past. It's used. With that in mind, you should be able to comfortably walk into any antiques shop with confidence. Most antiques dealers are eager to give a history lesson on a given piece, style, or period. If history is not your driving interest and you are intent on addressing a specific furniture need, reinventing an antique should not present a moral dilemma.

Often it is presumed that antiques are expensive. This can be so, but there are a variety of treasures to be found at all price ranges, especially if you're creative enough to envision alternative uses or willing to undertake some restoration. Approach antiques shops in earnest as you would an art museum. You're not necessarily going to buy; rather, you want to learn.

As you're shopping, if a piece of furniture really attracts you and you think you would like to buy it, ask to take it home on approval. This is not an uncommon practice, though it varies among dealers. It allows you to see the piece in the actual space where you intend to use it. Dealers with whom you've established a purchasing relationship are often particularly amenable to this. Most are pleased to oblige with a credit card imprint.

Evaluate an antique by the interest it evokes. It may make you feel sentimental; perhaps it stirs a childhood memory. It may be from your favorite part of the world, or from a culture that intrigues you. My interest in antiques is history driven. How many stories have been told over this table before me, and how many will continue to be told long after me? On a general note, while antiques in pristine condition are more valuable, I personally prefer wear on a piece of furniture.

I don't care for things that are strictly decorative unless they have had an individual history or mark a bygone technology. Particularly interesting to me are tools—from ones for farming to medicine and navigation. Strict decoratives have the feeling of a theatrical prop. A Han dynasty figure that dates back to 200 B.C., by contrast, fascinates by its history.

OLD SHEET
MUSIC WAS
GIVEN NEW LIFE
WITH MODERN
FRAMING.

authentic details

Keep your eyes open for functional pieces; there's no substitute for old fire-place tools, for example. The weight, size, and wear of the shovel—the small details distinguish a home of character. This logic applies to everything, from door pulls to saltcellars.

making adjustments

Keep an open vision and don't be discouraged by chairs that don't necessarily sit perfectly or table heights that don't support your intended use. For instance, I once bought a beautifully patinated farm table that was too low for comfortable seating. By adding large white porcelain casters to the legs, I elevated the table to the necessary height. Often older tables present this challenge. If you are off by only an inch or an inch and a half, casters are an easy fix. Wheels allow you to move a table with ease. Another option would be to add block feet. Chair heights may be adjusted by the addition of wheels as well, and their seats can be contoured or elevated by upholstery.

Likewise, finishes that are not appealing at first glance may be altered, changing the entire character of a furniture piece. The obvious approach would be a coat of paint, which can produce incredible results. Conversely, you may discover a great natural finish if you have the object stripped.

A TIBETAN WHEEL BENEATH A FOUND SERIES OF INK DRAWINGS BY AN UNKNOWN ARTIST.

TOP: TWENTIETH-CENTURY WOOD CARVINGS MOUNTED ON PLEXIGLAS.

ABOVE: A MAP OF UNKNOWN AGE ADDS PATINA TO A ROOM.

Large sets of vintage or antique dining chairs are very hard to come by. I once needed twelve chairs to complete a space. I wanted the patina of age, but finding something appropriate was proving challenging. Finally I came upon a large set of 1950s chinoiserie lacquered dining room chairs. They did not harmonize with the rest of the room in my client's house. The chairs as forms were beautiful, but the finish was a deterrent. I had them stripped to remove the black lacquer and Asian motifs. Without any refinishing, the stripping yielded a pale green, driftwood color from the saturated residue of the paint that the wood had permanently absorbed. The chairs took on a natural patina that was pleasing and suggestive of age. I cannot recommend the process to the risk averse, however, as I have had an occasional upset in this regard. If you're nervous about taking a chance, you might try this with pieces that are already chipped or worn enough to give a reasonable indication of what lies beneath.

The style of an object can sometimes be transformed with a coat of paint. I once had an otherwise unremarkable armoire refinished in a simple matte black paint. It turned out that the piece had extraordinary beadwork—recessed panels that had been lost to several coats of paint over the years. The black paint accentuated crisp geometric detail; the nondescript armoire suddenly took on a sophisticated, modern sensibility.

the last word

Carefully search the recesses of an antiques shop for objects that may work for you once restored or used alternatively. In the end, when you add that storied antique to your home, you will have created something that will not be found elsewhere.

FORMERLY
FINISHED IN
A CHINOISERIE
STYLE, THIS
CHAIR WAS
STRIPPED TO
ITS ORIGINAL
FINISH.

THE WHITE
ENAMEL METAL
SHADE ON THIS
PENDANT IS
RESPECTFUL OF
THE FINE ART IN
THIS SPARE
ENVIRONMENT.

10 light

aim for subtle illumination

I began formulating my design aesthetic early on, sometime between learning to crawl and learning to walk. According to my mother, I was opinionated from the beginning. My first word was "light." I was probably complaining that there was too much. By the time I was eight, I had accumulated enough savings to purchase a lamp. I brought it home on my bicycle. A second trip was required to retrieve its shade. Later, the lamp would undergo a series of makeovers in my capable hands. The bamboo relief would be highlighted with sepia brushstrokes; the shade would melt if you actually turned on the light because it had been covered in several coats of different colored candle wax. What my poor parents endured; few fates could be as costly as the creative child. I learned that if you persist, paint applied by brush will adhere to almost anything.

All kidding aside, lighting remains one of the most challenging elements of designing a home. Nothing defines atmosphere more than lighting. From the primitive candle to the modern recessed light, sensitivity to this is as important as the warp and weft of textiles and the selection of furniture pieces. Lighting will affect their final presentation and ultimately the ease of the space. Therefore, lighting selection should be considered thoughtfully.

True to my youthful instincts, I still don't like a lot of bright light. I remember arriving at a friend's house for a party and seeing that unflattering light was at full glare. I remained frozen in the vestibule as long as I could without being rude, then sprinted out to the balcony, where many other guests had gravitated toward the darkness. I am such a believer in dimmers that I use them in closets and on exterior lighting. No place in the home requires a glaring beacon.

There is an otherwise great restaurant that I won't go to because it has pin lights over every table. This would make anyone self-conscious and is unforgiving of the slightest water spot on tableware. Soft illumination from ambient or atmospheric sources is far more pleasing and flattering. Brighten a room by lighting the face of a bookshelf with picture lights rather than placing a lamp directly behind a sofa. A peripheral light source is more atmospheric.

FORMER
FACTORY
LIGHTS ARE
SUSPENDED
FROM METAL
UTILITY PIPES.

In spite of my penchant for ambient light, in heavy work areas such as kitchens, it is critical that form follow function. For nighttime reading, use specific task lighting such as bedside wall-mounted lamps with elbows. I doubt that I've placed a single bed without a pair of functional swing-arm fixtures with dimmers and individual switches to accommodate different habits.

When you display art, picture lights should be discreet. Remember, the intention is to illuminate the art, rather than to draw attention to the fixture.

Billiard lighting may provide another option. Billiard lights are horizontal pendant fixtures with two distinct light sources at either end. These present a great alternative to a traditional lamp over a desk, a library table, a dining room table, or a sofa table at a room's center. Mounted over a kitchen island, they can subdue the visual void that islands often create. Dual pendants may interestingly punctuate the void. In a more modern setting, metal utilitarian industrial pendants may be appropriate. In a more traditional setting, hanging reclaimed milk-glass schoolhouse pendants may solve the challenge.

You may want to find something less predictable, in which case it will be challenging to locate pairs. During your search, look for flush-mounted dome fixtures, which are commonly found in multiples. These might work with some minor alteration and the addition of a decorative chain to convert them into pendants. Pendants offer a nice finishing touch elsewhere in the home as well, such as a diminutive crystal fixture in a small powder room or an adolescent's bedroom.

Whenever possible, having multiple light sources on multiple switches is an ideal way to control atmosphere for varying functions.

AN INDUSTRIAL
FIXTURE SERVES AS
TASK LIGHTING
WITHOUT BEING
VISUALLY IMPOSING.

simple chandeliers

When it comes to pendant light fixtures, simplicity should be the objective. Celebrate the dinner guests, not the chandelier. One way to calm an ornate crystal chandelier is to remove some of its crystal. Likewise, try to avoid ornate switch plates. Buy simple switch plates that can be painted to match the wall color.

When searching for chandeliers, explore architectural salvage yards in addition to traditional resources. Sometimes you will find old pendants and other light fixtures that can be easily revitalized with new electrical wiring and perhaps the addition of decorative pendant lamp shades.

My clients often ask me about the right height to hang a pendant fixture. Generally speaking, as I've said, they should be hung so that they do not interfere visually or physically with interaction between those seated. A good rule of thumb is to hang a chandelier about 30 inches above a table's surface. This works unless, of course, you have NBA clients, or clients who have NBA guests!

Avoid bare bulbs on pendant lamps and chandeliers; they cast unflattering light. Instead, add small metal or paper shades to soften harsh light. Select small clip-on lamp shades lined in white paper. Shades with interior color may cast that color, affecting the surrounding walls and textiles. On the subject of luminous surfaces, a solid brass chandelier may become less conspicuous if it is oxidized. One word of caution: only solid brass can be oxidized.

spark your own illumination

My fascination with redefining objects extends to lighting. I have had exterior porch lanterns oxidized for interior use. I have also had antique oil-burning coach lanterns electrified for modern use. Likewise, most vases and urns can be converted into modern lamps. If you come across a porcelain vase that you like, consider taking it to a good lamp repair shop, where they may be able to adapt it into a more interesting lamp.

candlelight

I like very tall candlesticks that don't obstruct sight lines while creating atmosphere. A wrought-iron antique champagne caddy can become a beautiful candlestick. When placing candles, light them before your guests arrive to achieve wax accumulation, which looks inviting. Imperfection is a sign of life. Line your walkway with candlelit hurricanes. This will set the stage for an intimate gathering.

I once had clients who insisted upon using peripheral candlelight to produce the atmosphere they desired in their dining room. Two small children precluded the use of candles on the table. This was an unusual but surmountable challenge. It was simply a matter of finding the appropriate sconce pieces. I found candle stands with upright candleholders that I had rotated and retrofitted to work as mounted wall sconces. These unusual sconces use real candles, yet they are out of the reach of harm's way.

A PAINTED
LAMP DEPICTS
A WORN
LANDSCAPE
SCENE.

If there is not an adequate ambient light source, candles are always pleasing, particularly in a dining room. Other clients wanted a central pendant fixture to hang in their dining room in the country. All of the manufactured lighting I could find seemed contrived or overstated in this setting. Finally, I found a grain scale, piled it up with thick candles, and hung it over a large round table as an adjunct light source. This was a pleasing solution in this rural setting.

the last word

Develop an appreciation for subtle light from atmospheric sources, simple chandeliers, and candles. Carrying this sensibility throughout your home can bring soothing light to your space.

ART DOESN'T
HAVE TO BE
PRECIOUS. ONE
OF MY MOST
PRIZED PIECES
IS A DISCARDED
BARN DOOR
DISCOVERED
LEANING
AGAINST THE
SIDE OF A
CLOSED
AUCTION
HOUSE. THE
BLACK
SILHOUETTE OF
A HORSE ON THE
PRIMITIVE DOOR
IS REMARKABLY
MODERN. AFTER
CONSIDERABLE
EFFORT, I
TRACKED DOWN
THE OWNER,
AND $50 LATER,
IT WAS MINE.

11 relate

select evocative art,
and frame it with style

Art—in all its possible forms—should move you. It should certainly be more than atmospheric. It should have emotional consequence. Whether a multimillion-dollar canvas or a twenty-dollar flea-market print, it should make you smile, laugh, think, or reflect. Even if it is simply color on a canvas, it should be evocative. I have a large modern canvas in my dining room that I commissioned with the simplest composition: two vivid slices of color—yellow and orange. It casts an extraordinary glow throughout the day and is literally radiant at night. These colors represent warmth for me.

It's important to thoughtfully invest time and emotion in the selection of art. Not enough interest is taken here, which I imagine

165

INTRICATELY
CARVED CORBELS
SUPPORT A
LIMESTONE SHELF,
WHICH SUPPORTS
A RARE HAN
DYNASTY FIGURE.

accounts for the proliferation of bland, emotionless art that is often treated as obligatory filler in the home. Art should not simply be bought as decoration. Rather it should be contemplated independently. If buying mass-produced art, look for innovative composition and mix it up. Place the more painterly abstract opposite a sepia map.

Choose a few meaningful pieces. Have a black-and-white photo of your dog enlarged. This will no doubt make you smile at each passing. As you begin to acquire art, keep emerging artists in mind; support your local art community when possible.

I recently assisted a friend in selecting art for his home. Dear though he is, this was a laborious process. He was far more invested in the construction phase. Art was not a priority. This is not new; so many interiors completely fall down here.

It is astounding to me how someone can fastidiously undertake an interior-design project and treat something as visually present as art with indifference. We had worked so hard on this environment, and my friend was going to hang filler on the walls, some of which dated back to his college years. Fortunately our friendship allowed me to be candid with him to a degree that is not always possible with clients.

Once we survived this hurdle, we had to get past the presumption that art had to be expensive. We settled on a collection of black-and-white pinhole photography, the subject matter of which was completely appealing to both of us. Ironically, I recently heard that the photographer in question had a retrospective at a respected museum in Washington, D.C. The photography, as it turned out, was valuable. This emphasizes a very critical point: Buy what you like. I have actually made some inadvertent good investments with this outlook.

A SEPIA OIL IS ALMOST INDISCERNIBLE FROM THE ANTIQUE STONE OF THE FIREPLACE.

display art imaginatively

In addition to hanging art on walls, consider other options for presentation. Art can and should be interactive where possible.

Be on the lookout for would-be art display alternatives as you shop for furniture pieces. Don't disregard solutions just because they are imperfect. A peeling veneer, faded paint, or an otherwise failing finish can often be redeemed by a simple lacquer spray paint. Black or white paint can often revitalize a neglected piece. As I've said, the intention, after all, is to provide focal presence for the art, not for the piece the art is displayed on.

Just as the subject matter of an art piece should captivate, its method of display may further engage interaction. Leaning art is an alternative to hanging it. This can enhance the presence that an art piece assumes and, depending upon the art medium, can relate a three-dimensional quality. Explore placement such as a landing at the top of a staircase, where the art will unveil itself as you approach. If you're leaning art against a wall in a precarious place, secure it discreetly with a hook and wire. Leaning art is also a solution for those who are not decisive about permanent place-ment. This method may become a necessity. Plaster walls are often difficult to anchor hooks into. Depending on the size of the art, additional placement options throughout the home will unfold. Even the back of a floating sofa may suit.

presentation

Consider placing art at the viewer's eye level when seated. Experiment and hang or lean it on a bookshelf. From this vantage you may discover that you are more likely to study the art, where once it might have gone unnoticed. There is no rule you must follow when hanging or displaying art. The goal is to create an environment in which the art will be appreciated.

EVERY ROOM
CAN BENEFIT
FROM ART.

SMALL PINHOLE
PHOTOGRAPHY
BECOMES FOCAL
WITH OVERSIZE
MATTING.

Limited wall space should not quell a would-be collector's appetite. Art can find a home in many untraditional venues, such as furniture with ratcheted adjustable tops, including music stands, book rests, lecterns, or architects' tables. Place art on top of a pile of books on a coffee table. Low pedestals provide options for displaying both sculpture or small canvases where wall space is at a premium. Art displayed in this manner encourages study, perhaps more so than art predictably stationed in a hallway. These methods of display will generally accommodate smaller works, which might be lost on an expansive wall.

Decorative folding screens offer another opportunity for suspending paintings or drawings. Or a single floating shelf suspended from a wall is a very respectful way to honor a sculpture or a leaning art piece.

You need not limit your displays to what is thought to be traditional art. Art in its most base interpretation need only stimulate the senses of the beholder. This greatly broadens the possibilities. I personally am intrigued by industrial machine parts. They are not unlike the primitive objects so often displayed in modern environments. A wall of suspended antique printing or wallpaper blocks can make an interesting composition.

A neutral room palette is a natural backdrop for art. I've been true to this philosophy in all of my homes. A warm white has been my color of choice, as it is respectful of art.

SURROUND
YOURSELF
WITH ART,
WHETHER A
MEANINGFUL
SCULPTURE
OR A
DELICATE
FOUND
SKETCH.

art as architecture

My affection for art is such that it has transcended the obvious place-ment on a wall. Recently I commissioned an art piece that was engi-neered as a sliding wall. The wall itself was the art. These sliding doors were a modern, monochromatic, translucent mosaic constructed of white shards of melded hand-fired porcelain. Light passes through this composition, casting the most extraordinary shadows. The texture on the reverse side suggests freshly troweled clay. This textural composi-tion is suggestive of a modern stained-glass window.

framing and matting art

Art may assume more presence if it is framed importantly. To enhance focal quality, I often use substantial matting around art pieces to draw greater attention to the subject matter. A simple mat can be a foil for a heavily carved frame, imposing a modern sensibility. A large white mat beckons you into a faint primitive pencil drawing in an ornately carved frame. You don't want to go too minimalist when it comes to matting, however; in fact, a small mat or the absence of any matting may pro-duce the opposite effect, distracting from the art piece, which suddenly competes with the frame.

As you consider framing, you don't necessarily need an expensive new frame. While antiquing, no doubt you will come across framed artwork that lacks appeal. It may be worth the purchase to salvage the frame. Don't be put off by frames that are larger than the art piece you are considering framing; they can easily be cut down to size by an art framer. You may in fact find yourself with adequate framing for two art pieces, or perhaps a small mirror frame may be born of the rem-nants. A glass purveyor can customize a mirror to suit your frame at little cost.

A FLOATING SHELF
DISPLAYS A HAN
DYNASTY FIGURE.

A LANDSCAPE
PAINTING PLACED ON
BARE WHITE WALLS
ENGAGES WITHOUT
DISTRACTING.

Don't disregard existing art pieces if they have sentimental value. One couple I worked with had a collection of oil paintings by a regional artist. The work was moody, and each of them had coincidentally collected this relatively obscure artist before they were married. At first glance, the artwork was unremarkable because it was overwhelmed by bright, newly fabricated gilt framing. This negated the subtlety and credibility of the work. I had been through the house on several occasions, but I hadn't paid much attention to this peripheral hall art. One day the owner shared a catalog of the artist's work—unframed. Even reproduced in a catalog, the art was extraordinary. This led me to thoughtfully revisit its presentation. In the end, I had the art reframed with significant matting that drew the eye to its remarkable content. Art should always be presented with respect for the content. Often artworks are squeezed into their frames in such a way that they cannot be appreciated. Once again, respectful treatment places the emphasis on the art.

Forgoing a frame may enhance some art pieces. You might find a small canvas or an artist's proof that is too delicate in its composition for its frame. Unless the piece is valuable, or in need of protection from light, active children, or pets, leave it unframed and place it on a table where it can be thoroughly enjoyed.

USE MATTING TO UNIFY DISPARATE IMAGES AND FRAME THEM SIMILARLY TO CREATE VISUAL HARMONY.

incorporating technology

Technophiles may view their plasma screen as art; to each his own. I generally try to avoid the display of any audiovisual equipment. If having a television in a bedroom or a living room is essential, perhaps it can be concealed in an armoire or a recessed cavity in a wall with built-in pocket doors. An exposed plasma screen may in any event be entirely appropriate in a modern setting. Here the clean lines of an exposed screen may blend quietly into more streamlined architecture.

sentimental items

None of us is without cherished keepsakes. Sometimes sentimentality prevails over good taste. Generally, our own keepsakes are perfectly good; it is those of others that offend (so we think!). Every once in a while, however, you get lucky and a husband, wife, and designer agree that a keepsake should be displayed. In one instance, a client had collected wine labels from a vineyard that had sentimental meaning for her. She wanted to display them in her family room, which had very limited wall space. The perimeter of the room was punctuated by doors, openings, and built-ins.

Inspired by a document stand, I designed a low, slant-topped sofa table to flank the back of a sofa, which floated at the room's center. Three labels were framed as a single triptych, matted to delineate each image, then leaned on the slant-top.

A GUSTAVIAN CHAIR
AND AN ITALIAN MANTEL
ARE A DELICATE
COUNTERBALANCE TO
THE BOLD DONALD
SULTAN CANVAS.

combining tastes

A hallmark of my design is the juxtaposition of many styles, so when a client comes to me with a varied art collection, I enjoy the challenge of making sense out of its presentation. In one case, a couple's collection consisted of both modern and mannered early landscapes. In the living room, I leaned a modern canvas on the mantel. In the owners' bedroom, I removed a hunt portrait from its gilded frame, thereby lending it a more modern sensibility. This philosophy of mixing enhanced the interiors of the entire home.

Remember to keep an open mind as you consider art for your home. I often accompany clients on art trips. I usually go ahead of them, editing the possibilities within an overwhelming and generally infinite universe. One shopping trip is particularly memorable because my clients and I went to a gallery with the intention of looking at large canvases with singular gestures of bold color. Instead, we walked away with small black-and-white photography, which ended up being a more suitable fit for the space.

A LOW PLATFORM SUPPORTS AN ABSTRACT RAM SCULPTURE.

CONSIDER A
HAND-PAINTED
CHINESE ARMOIRE
AS ART.

the last word

Art is essential for personal expression and definition in any
environment. Lean art, display it on a small easel, attach it to
a shelf of a bookcase, suspend it from a screen, or lay it on a
coffee table. The possibilities are endless even with limited
wall space.

AN OPEN FLOOR
PLAN IS MADE MORE
INTIMATE WITH
MOVING MULTIMEDIA
PORCELAIN ART
PANELS BY ARTIST
MARGARET BOOZER.

TANG DYNASTY HORSES CIRCA A.D. 700 CONTRAST WITH A MODERN CANVAS.

12 focus

collect with an eye toward visual harmony

When it comes to collecting and displaying objects, remember these two concepts: "opposites distract" and "like-kind." Editing your belongings and placing them with care can heighten visual interest while creating calm in an environment. A visual harmony emerges when similar objects are placed together in a contained area, bookshelf, exposed cupboard, or china hutch. By *similar,* I am referring to an immediate family of objects that share the same purpose, general form, and color. Objects such as collectible china that is bought by the individual piece should be of the same color, whether mulberry transferware or Staffordshire flow blue. An assortment of patterns within one of these groups usually looks very attractive when displayed

A WALL OF SHALLOW SHELVES WAS DESIGNED TO DISPLAY A COLLECTION OF NINETEENTH-CENTURY FLOW BLUE.

together, but staying within the color grouping and pattern density is the safest way to assure visual harmony rather than clutter, especially when you're just starting out. In this example, you could look for a variety of shapes as this lends depth and layer to a display.

A sensitive, logical approach to scale also leads to more successful display. Graceful gradation of scale can present beautifully. You should avoid placing objects together that appear distinctly odd next to each other, such as a small dessert plate next to a soup tureen or a large platter. If a collection such as porcelains can be displayed in a layered fashion, place the larger pieces at the rear of the display cabinet and graduate the size to the smallest at the cabinet's front. An ironstone collection (shown on page 23) illustrates this point. Dozens of pieces placed together—unusual pitchers, bowls, platters, plates, and cake stands on a baker's rack—relate due to the similar qualities of color, curve of line, and size. While there are a number of varied shapes among these objects, because of these shared qualities, they read as one quiet sculpture in the collective. The composition appears to be singular, uninterrupted by divergent colors or pattern. Flow blue, creamware, pewter, bone, and ivory cutlery all follow suit in their collective presentation. My preference for grouping similar objects extends to tableware and settings. Flatware patterns do

AN UNUSUAL COLLECTION OF BROWN-AND-WHITE TAKOU FILLS A PAINTED CABINET.

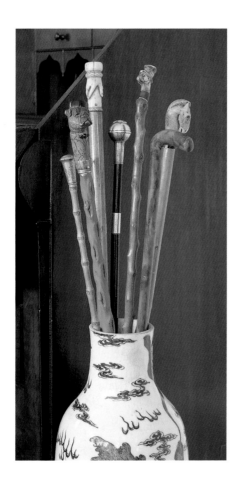

not need to match, but the medium—pewter, silver, bone—should always be the same, ideally of similar weight and scale. In other words, only place pewter with pewter of a similar patina. Likewise, if the flatware is weighty, with a substantial handle, for example, the other integrated pieces should share this quality.

You may very well have an inadvertent collection accumulating in a random decorative box or a drawer, or on a remote shelf in a closet. What often defines a collection is grouping similar objects thoughtfully. It is not uncommon that I find myself in an antiques shop carefully examining a given object when the dealer approaches and asks, "Do you collect?" Inevitably, I pause. If I answer in the affirmative, this suggests I know something about the object at hand. Even if I know nothing about the object, my pause buys time to "step up" and answer "Yes" with some level of confidence in order to open a comfortable dialogue. I am certain I am not alone in this regard. The truth is there are objects I routinely collect as second nature. I have piles of flow blue, ironstone, and antique cutlery, and at least several precious Han dynasty figures. The very act of accumulating objects qualifies one to some unwitting degree as a collector.

Look around your home. There may be an opportunity for cautious assembly. The objects should be attractive and of interest by some standard. Placing them together may make them more interesting to study by virtue of their difference. In any event, don't be discouraged if you find you don't have anything worthy of display; this discovery is far better than forcing the issue and reaching to feature some valueless collection of lint-covered stray buttons. If you find yourself short on display items, view this as an opportunity to learn and shop. The subject of your collection is of course quite personal. It may be the history or craft that intrigues. For some it may be the thrill of finding more of the obscure. Perhaps the objects are simply visually appealing. I have seen collections from the broad to the obscure: labels, maps, taxidermy, shells, walking sticks (a personal favorite), primitive tools, primitive weapons . . . the possibilities are endless.

ANTIQUE
PEWTER
PLATES AND
CUTLERY TOP
A CARRARA
COUNTER.

CHINESE GREEN
VESSELS
GROUPED
TOGETHER MAKE
A GRAPHIC
PRESENTATION.

I enjoy collecting vintage mechanical objects such as marine sextants, scales, ladders, maps, and globes—the kinds of things that suit a gentleman's library. Antique globes on my library table inspire comments from others and recall my own travels, on which I found many of these pieces. They therefore hold fond memories. Be selective by editing and choosing only favorite objects for display. Collect objects that intrigue. For the cook, a collection of cutting boards, for instance, can represent a pleasing mix of different textures, woods, and shapes. Avoid impulsive collecting, which often translates into future clutter. Aim for harmony. In order for a collection to present meaningfully, there should be enough interesting objects placed together to inspire curiosity about the grouping.

displaying books

If books are your interest, these too can be displayed in various contexts. For instance, I prefer to pile books in a relaxed manner in the foyer of my country house rather than have them perfectly placed on bookshelves. The purpose of this house is to provide calm and respite. I instantly associate that with escaping into a great book. When choosing books, I took visiting friends into account, adding volumes on art, history, and architecture as well as a variety of bipartisan political biographies. The goal was to create a small library of books that could indulge every interest.

While the selection of books in a home is often random, their presentation can truly affect comfort within a space. Books lined rigidly on a shelf may cause apprehension. You may be hesitant to pull one out and mess up the arrangement. By contrast, with books in accessible disarray, you're more prone to grab one. Having books randomly placed throughout the home can make them more inviting to read.

displaying photographs

Family photographs, a staple, present one of my most recurrent challenges. So much is revealed just in the discussion about how they should be displayed, in what part of the home, and which side of the family should go where. Dozens of unrelated photographs, some in color, others in black and white or sepia, in frames with incongruous sizes, shapes, and finishes, quickly take on the appearance of clutter, blurring their content. In some cases, I've reproduced collections of photography in black and white or sepia and framed them all in $\frac{1}{8}$-inch-wide black or white wood or metal frames. Each photograph was matted uniformly to be the same size regardless of the size of the photographs. A collection treated this way can hang beautifully in a corridor or a stairwell.

A MIDCENTURY
PRINT ON A
SUSPENDED
SHALLOW LEDGE
ADDS INTEREST
TO A REMOTE
HALLWAY.

ANTIQUE WOODEN
TRIVETS AND
CUTTING BOARDS
CAN BE USED FOR
HORS D'OEUVRES.

A COLLECTION
OF ANTIQUE HORN
AND STERLING
MAGNIFYING
GLASSES MAKES
A HANDSOME
DISPLAY.

I once used a vitrine, in this instance, a small glass-topped tea-height table with an exposed interior drawer, to display family photographs. Placed as a living room side table, the vitrine kept the interior landscape of the living room visually calm, while at the same time accommodating the display of important keepsakes.

Color photographs can be similarly addressed, but I would suggest that all photographs displayed together be of the same size and framed in the same medium. Color photographs of varied composition create visual competition. Since the intent is to unify a collection, this visual dissimilarity may be calmed by using smaller examples instead of images that are the standard 4 by 6 inches or larger.

Collections can be very thoughtfully treated if they are considered during the initial design phase of a project. During a renovation project, I once removed walls beneath a suspended stair, which exposed a bare wall beyond the now optically floating stair. This wall became the focal point of the kitchen as you entered. It provided a perfect opportunity for the construction of shallow platter display shelving, which beautifully accommodated a collection of blue-and-white porcelain (shown on page 186).

the last word

Remember to group similar objects together so they read as one. Visual harmony equals calm. As you contemplate your collection, take as much care in developing its proper display as you do in choosing the pieces.

A TAVERN BENCH
PROVIDES
ALTERNATIVE
SEATING AT THE
NINETEENTH-
CENTURY
GATELEG TABLE.

13 invite

create child-friendly and forgiving environments

Designing homes with children in mind has changed dramatically over the last several years. When I grew up, parts of the house were off-limits. Today, few parents cordon off their homes. Plan accordingly for kids on a free rein. Using synthetic fabrics, commercial-grade carpets, and softly rounded corners makes it far less challenging to create durable and comfortable environments that are also attractive. What is child-friendly and forgiving? Ultrasuedes and vinyls that easily pass for genuine suedes and leathers. Some of these textiles feel remarkably like the real thing. Add to this the variety of outdoor fabrics that can be used indoors and you quickly discover that you don't have to sacrifice style for durability. For the most part, these

CURVES ARE
KID-FRIENDLY.

synthetics are stain and soil resistant. Many of these textiles meet high-traffic commercial standards.

As much as I promote these new synthetics, they are often greeted with skepticism. Now that public spaces are increasingly expected to have the feeling of a residential environment, commercial manufacturers have responded with more and more attractive textiles. "My kids will stain anything" is not an uncommon sentiment among my clients. "Let's see how well these miracle fabrics stand up to ketchup, grape juice, and chocolate." More than one client has smeared chocolate on samples of Ultrasuede. Wiping it with soap and water cleaned it instantly. Vinyl is also an option that convincingly passes for leather. With vinyl, white upholstery and children can coexist.

On a more immediate and practical note, there is concern as children are given greater rein about the house. The parents of two small children, fearful of the inevitable food and beverage spills, naturally wanted practical textiles on the furniture, as well as durable floor coverings. I covered the sofas in the family room with pale putty–colored Ultrasuede. I used vinylized natural linen on the Gustavian side dining chairs and a cream vinyl that passed for kidskin leather on the head wing chairs. The floors are covered in commercial-grade carpet, which relieved some of the concerns about food and beverage stains. I use vinyl in some of the high-traffic areas of my own home.

Noncommercial fabrics such as linen and cotton can be vinylized. I have used this treatment successfully on dining room chairs and kitchen banquettes. For high-use areas, the addition of the protective coating makes fabrics resistant to liquid spills. Of course, if you're having a soft supple fabric vinylized, you may be compromising its hand, but in the long run, considering all the spills of childhood, the trade-off may be worth the sacrifice.

If sharp table edges are a concern, an alternative way to execute an attractive coffee or sofa table is with upholstery. A simple Parsons-style with eased edges will easily accommodate this treatment.

DURABLE CUBES
MAKE ATTRACTIVE
KID-FRIENDLY
SEATING.

CHILDREN'S ROOMS INCREASINGLY TAKE ON LESS EXPECTED PALETTES.

twenty-first-century synthetics

Consider outdoor textiles as an alternative for interior rooms. Today's outdoor fabrics contrast greatly with those of the past. Not long ago, almost all outdoor textiles were heavy and coarse to the touch, particularly in the water-repellant varieties. Today, however, some of the outdoor fabrics are as sumptuous as their indoor counterparts. It's hard to imagine, but many of these new textiles don't absorb water or mildew. Interior slipcovering in these forgiving textiles is great if you have kids. Children and pets can have a field day on furniture with slipcovers, which preserve a more delicate fabric beneath to be revealed only for adult entertaining. High-tech tweed, bouclé, and woven fabrics designed to withstand the elements can bear the brunt of most childhood calamities.

Ease of care is another advantage of these textiles. Most can be maintained with a damp cloth immediately following an accident. Many of the new synthetics are even machine washable. These textiles present practical choices for high-traffic upholstery such as family-room sofas and kitchen chairs. The varieties available—from a simple grain to mock ostrich—will suit any taste. From upholstered cubes in playrooms to dog beds, all these forgiving and attractive options can be tastefully integrated with any palette.

let your home grow with you

With children in the home, you might consider graduating your purchases. Buy pieces consistent with a child's stage of development that may later be used in a secondary room as the children mature and furniture options become greater. For example, draperies can be yanked from their rods, so you might want to consider retractable window shades. These can later be embellished with draperies when such curiosity moves elsewhere.

durable flooring

Pay attention to what's underfoot, as well. Choose durable, attractive commercial carpeting for high-traffic areas, such as staircases and family rooms. Carpet tiles make good sense in play areas. Minor stains can be cleaned, and if a tile is permanently damaged, you can substitute a new one without having to replace the entire carpet. I recommend buying extra tiles if you go this route just in case the style you buy is no longer available when you need to replace them. Surprisingly, felt is also very forgiving; certain varieties can literally be sanded clean. On the carpet-tile front, you and your children can have fun creating your own mosaic. Think of the floors as art. Rubber tile provides another option for kid-proofing an area. Rubber tiles can cushion a fall, and they help absorb some noise. Woven vinyls with sponge backing may be an interim replacement for sisal or flat wovens in a play area. Many of them are both stain and water resistant, making them more practical than their jute counterparts.

MARK CAMERON
BOYD CREATED
THIS CANVAS
TO INVITE
INTERACTION.

THE LITTLE ONE
WAS COMMIS-
SIONED TO CREATE
THIS FREESTYLE
CANVAS. HER PLAY
WAS LIMITED TO
BLACK INK. THANK
GOODNESS FOR
PARENTS WILLING
TO INDULGE THEIR
DESIGNER.

children's bedrooms

One dramatic change I have noticed in decorating is the treatment of children's bedrooms with gender neutrality. Many parents are choosing non-traditional colors for their children's rooms; in fact many mothers are adamant that their daughters not have rooms in formerly expected colors. Children themselves are becoming increasingly involved in the color selection, a task once the sole provenance of adults. I have been surprised on more than one occasion by children with refreshingly sophisticated taste. I once had clients who wanted to extend a midcentury aesthetic into a nursery. I painted the baby's bedroom mustard and applied graphite-colored decals on the walls. The walls were reminiscent of an abstract canvas, which intrigued their child while maintaining the sensibility of the rest of the home. Creating this relationship seems to be a trend.

Together with the wealth of kid-friendly textiles, there is a burgeoning market in what is best characterized as miniature adult furniture, from Victorian to modern.

As much as I like to keep things tidy with kids, sometimes I think they ought to be free to play in paint. In lieu of commemorative child portraits, I encourage recording their state of mind as they evolve. A child's early expression may be captured in ink on paper. This free association produces some very appealing visuals that are worthy of framing. Abstract artwork carefully choreographed by parental supervision may be more inspired than a family portrait or a bronzed baby shoe.

I suggested such an application to some progressive clients who wanted something other than a staid family portrait in their dining room. They made a huge triptych of their three adolescent sons' handprints: three large canvases were stretched, one yellow panel for orange handprints, one gray panel for green handprints, and a blue one for purple handprints. Each of the three panels was dedicated to one of the three children, creating an indelible memory and an unexpected interpretation of a family portrait.

updated recreation rooms

As with the rest of the house, a new level of sophistication abounds in unconventional recreation spaces. Top a Parsons table with cork and dedicate one wall to a large framed chalkboard. The kids can constantly update it with their interpretation of art, resulting in an interactive chalkboard. Now, among the myriad paint options, there are chalkboard paints and magnetic paints useful for avoiding puncturing walls. The ever-changing art of adolescence can now be changed with a magnet. Wall paints have also become forgiving. Traditionally, when you washed a matte-finish paint, the paint would dull and leave an impression. Now washable matte-finish paints mean that at long last, children can comfortably take over the white home with abandon.

the last word

Today's high-tech indoor/outdoor fabrics, commercial-grade carpets, and design-savvy children make it possible for your home to be both kid-friendly and stylish.

14 relax

know when to stop

By now, you have studied your home and discovered what appeals to you. You may have painted the walls in a procession of soft color washes to subtly unify the room palettes. Perhaps you have introduced layers of texture or reupholstered a formerly "off-limits" silk-covered chair with a durable, user-friendly fabric so you and your children can enjoy the chair without worry. You may have gone antiquing and found a number of interesting objects that will lend character to each room.

You finally have a home that suits your lifestyle. Know when to stop. It's all right to have a bare wall. Not every square inch of a room has to be covered.

A room is complete when you are called to it for respite. If, while still stuck in bumper-to-bumper traffic on your drive home from a long workday, you see relief ahead in the form of a chair in a particular room, perhaps with a good book or a glass of wine, you have finished.